La Statira

The Textual Sources,
with a Documentary Postscript

Ill. 1. Frontispiece of the printed libretto of *La Statira*, Rome, 1690 (Bologna, Civico Museo Bibliografico-Musicale).

La Statira
by Pietro Ottoboni
and Alessandro Scarlatti

The Textual Sources,
with a Documentary Postscript

William C. Holmes

Monographs in Musicology No. 2

PENDRAGON PRESS

NEW YORK

Other Titles in the Series:

Analysis and Value Judgement by Carl Dahlhaus,
translated by Siegmund Levarie (1983) No. 1

Arts, Sciences, Alloys by Iannis Xenakis, translated
by Sharon Kanach (in press) No. 3

Alessandro Scarlatti's Gli equivoci nel sembiante:
The History of a Baroque Opera by Frank D'Accone
(in press) No. 4

Library of Congress Cataloging In Publication Data

Holmes, William, 1928-
    La Statira by Pietro Ottoboni and Alessandro
Scarlatti.

    (Pendragon Press monographs in musicology
series ; 2)
    Bibliography: p.
    1. Scarlatti, Alessandro, 1660-1725. Statira.
I. Title. II. Series.
ML410.S22H6   1982   782.1'092'4   82-12357
ISBN 0-918728-18-5

Contents

For Donald J. Grout

Illustrations

La Statira

*The Textual Sources,
with a Documentary Postscript*

Introduction

By the year 1689, Roman society had been in the doldrums for some time. The pope, Innocent XI Odescalchi (reg. 1676-1689) was a conservative and during his pontificate public secular entertainments of all kinds had been kept to a minimum. Rome's largest theater, the Tordinona, had been closed in late 1674, ostensibly to prepare for the jubilee that was to be celebrated in 1675. In fact—probably because of Innocent's opposition to public performances—the theater did not reopen until after his rule had ended.[1] Innocent died on August 12, 1689. By October 6 of that year, the conclave had elected a new pope: Pietro Ottoboni, who took the name of Alexander VIII (reg. 1689-1691). The new pope, a member of a wealthy, powerful Venetian family, had always enjoyed the secular arts. Thus he lost no time in showing the Romans that, during his pontificate, many of the social glories of the earlier seventeenth century would be restored. He was also quick to reinstate the time-honored practice of nepotism. Hardly had Alexander VIII ascended the papal throne when he called two of his Venetian nephews into his service. Marco was made cardinal

[1] The standard study on this theater and its history is A. Cametti, *Il Teatro Tordinona poi di Apollo*, 2 vols. (Tivoli, 1938).

3

and became Castellano di S. Angelo, Generale delle Galere, and Duca di Fiano. His brother Antonio was given the title of Principe di Soglio and Generale della Chiesa. On November 7, 1689, Pietro Ottoboni, son of Antonio and grandnephew of the pope, was made cardinal and Vice Cancelliere della Chiesa.

Young Pietruccio (1667-1740)—as he was sometimes called to distinguish him from his granduncle, the pope—was the last and perhaps the most famous member of his family. From the age of 22, when he became cardinal, until his death, he used his immense power and wealth to support the arts, especially music and the theater. Within six months after receiving his cardinal's hat, Pietro had not only commissioned Alessandro Scarlatti to set a libretto he himself had written, but also had added Arcangelo Corelli to his household rolls as principal musician.[2] Cardinal Ottoboni's official residence at the palace of the Cancelleria, the basilica of San Lorenzo in Damaso adjacent to it, and the Tordinona theater, which he reopened, soon became active centers for some of the most splendid musical and theatrical performances held in seventeenth-century Rome.

Cardinal Ottoboni did not content himself with being merely a patron of the arts; he was an active participant throughout his life. He fancied himself a poet of no mean accomplishment—a self-judgement with which contemporary critics did not always agree. He was an active member of the Arcadian Academy, under the pseudonymn of Crateo Pradelini. In addition to supporting the Tordinona theater, he was responsible for the construction of a private theater in the Cancelleria. During his long life, Ottoboni wrote masses of poetry, many librettos for oratorios, *feste teatrali*, and other entertainments. As a young man, he also wrote five secular opera librettos: *L'amante del suo nemico* (music by F. C. Lanciani, Rome, 1688); *La Statira* (music by A. Scarlatti, Rome, 1690); *Amore e gratitudine* (music by F. C. Lanciani, Rome,

---

[2] The basic work on Cardinal Ottoboni and music is H. J. Marx, "Die Musik am Hofe Pietro Ottobonis unter Arcangelo Corelli," in *Studien zur Italienische-Deutschen Musikgeschichte* [*Analecta Musicologica*], V (Graz and Rome, 1968), pp. 104-177. See also S. H. Hansell, "Orchestral Practice at the Court of Cardinal Pietro Ottoboni," in *Journal of the American Musicological Society*, XIX (Fall, 1966), pp. 398-403.

1690); *Il Colombo ossia l'India scoperta* (composer unknown, Rome, 1691); and *La Forza dell' innocenza* (unfinished, 1690?).[3] *La Statira* opened the carnival season of 1690. The performances of the opera at the Tordinona theater were the first held there in fifteen years.

Before we proceed to the text of *La Statira* we should mention the musical sources of the opera. The complete music of *La Statira* is contained in each of four orchestral scores, all copied within twenty years of the opera's composition. These scores are now found at Munich, London, Cardiff, and Modena. There are also modern copies of the Munich score at Brussels and Dresden. The Library of Congress has a modern copy of the London score. With few exceptions, all of the surviving contemporary scores agree quite closely with one another—a situation not often encountered with opera scores of the seventeenth century. The important differences among these sources will be mentioned during the course of this study.

The Munich score (Bayrische Staatsbibliothek, Mus. Ms. 144) is a sumptuous volume in oblong format, bound in red leather with decorative gold stamping. On both the front and back of the binding appear the coat of arms of the Ottoboni family. The score lacks a title and the opening sinfonia. In 1977, the manuscript was given a new foliation. This score is the one that can be linked most closely with the early history of *La Statira*. Entries in the household accounts of Cardinal Ottoboni indicate that this score was probably the one copied by Tarquinio Lanciani (who may have been the brother of the composer Flavio Carlo).[4] Other entries in the account books show that Tarquinio also copied *Amore e gratitudine* and *Il Colombo*—the former, it will be recalled, set to music by Flavio Carlo.

The London score (British Library, Ms. add. 22.103) is of oblong format, and copied in a late-seventeenth-century hand. The

---

[3] For a list of Ottoboni's other works for the theater, including uncertain attributions, see Paul Kast, "Ottoboni, Pietro," in *Die Musik in Geschichte und Gegenwart*, vol. 10, cols. 487-90. See also H. J. Marx, "Ottoboni, Pietro," *The New Grove*, vol. 14, p. 28.

[4] Tarquinio's birth and death dates are not known, but he was on the payroll of the Ottoboni household from 1691 to 1693. He had copied music for the cardinal before this time, however. See Marx, op. cit., pp. 120, 170.

title page reads: "La Statira/Poesia del em:^{mo}Sig.^{r} Cardinale Otto-boni/Musica del Sig.^{r} Ales:^{o} Scarlatti." On the following page is written, "Purchase of C. Hamilton/12 Sept. 1857." The sinfonia contains many copying errors, including a nine-measure passage that makes no musical sense. This is the one score that does not include the music and text for the goddess Diana in the final scene of the opera.

The Cardiff score (Cardiff Public Library, Mackworth Collection) has an oblong format and is copied in a late-seventeenth-century hand. It contains no sinfonia. Within the large ornamental capital *N*[otte] that begins Act I is written, "La Statira del Sig. Aless.^{o} Scarlatti."

The score at Modena, (Biblioteca Estense, Ms. F. 1538) also oblong in format, is copied in a late-seventeenth-century hand. On the spine is written the title *Oronte*, which has been crossed out. Perhaps this score bears some connection to the earliest performances of *La Statira* in Rome, for a singer in the service of the Este, Antonio Borosini, sang the role of Oronte at these performances. On the title page is written in a nineteenth-century hand: "La Statira Autore incerto/Atti 3, con istromenti."

The most obvious major disagreement among the full scores of the opera is the lack of text and music for Diana in the final scene of the London score, as mentioned above. It might be supposed that because the text for Diana was added after the opera was finished (see below) and does not appear in the autograph libretto, the London score represents a version of the work closer to the original conception. This cannot be the case, however, for the London score includes other texts added to the opera. One might also surmise that economic considerations may have led to the deletion of Diana's scene from performances for which the London score was used. Her appearance requires an extra soprano, for all of the opera's characters are on stage when she enters. Such a hypothesis appears invalid, however, for the documents state that no expense was spared for the production of *La Statira* at the Tordinona theater. Another, more likely explanation is that the London score presents the opera as it was performed at the private theater in Ottoboni's residence at the Cancelleria, after Easter in 1690. The theater was small and could not have been equipped with the machinery necessary for Diana's appearance. The entrance of the goddess has nothing to do with the drama, and cutting it from a performance would not have detracted from the effectiveness of the denouement.

A number of aria collections contain some of the music of *La Statira*.[5] Three of these, one at Naples, another in the Vatican, and another at Paris, deserve special attention. The arias in the Naples collection differ in significant ways from the surviving complete scores, and several of the arias in the Vatican and Paris collections are ascribed to a composer other than Scarlatti. These three collections will be discussed later.

The libretto of *La Statira* is preserved in one printed edition and one working autograph:

Buagni. This is the single printed edition of the libretto. Its title page reads as follows:

> LA STATIRA/Dramma/per Musica/Recitato
> nel Teatro di/Torre di Nona./L'Anno
> 1690./Dedicato/ALLE DAME/di Roma./
> [Emblem]/Con licenza de' superiori./Si
> vendono in bottega di Francesco Leone/
> Libraro in Piazza Navona.

> LA STATIRA/Drama/for Music/Performed
> in the/Tordinona Theater./The Year
> 1690./Dedicated/TO THE LADIES/of Rome./
> [Emblem]/With permission of the authorities./
> Sold in the shop of Francesco Leone/
> Book dealer in Piazza Navona.

Rvat. This autograph is in the Biblioteca Apostolica Vaticana, Ottob. Lat. 2360. Its title page reads quite differently from that of the printed libretto: it does not mention the protagonist, is much extended, and has many cancellations (bracketed words are those crossed out in the manuscript):

---

[5] See G. Rostirolla's catalogue in R. Pagano and L. Bianchi, *Alessandro Scarlatti* (Turin, 1972), pp. 339-40.

LA
STATIRA
DRAMMA
PER MVSICA

Recitato nel Teatro di
Torre di Nona.

L'Anno 1690.

DEDICATO
ALLE DAME
DI ROMA:

In Roma, Per Gio:Francefco Buagni 1690.
Con licenza de' Superiori.

Si vendono in bottega di Francefco Leone
Libraro in Piazza Madama.

Ill. 2. Title page of the printed libretto of *La Statira*, Rome, 1690
(Bologna, Civico Museo Bibliografico-Musicale).

Virtù. Tempo. e Fortuna/Drama/Per/
Musica./[overo/Gl'Amori Fortunati/
di/Apelle] /overo/La Prencipessa [Romita]
Romita./L'Anno/1689/in/Roma.

Virtue, Time, and Fortune/Drama/for/
Music/[or/The Fortunate Loves/
of/Apelles]/or/ The Princess [Recluse]
Recluse./The Year/1689/in/ Rome.

A detailed comparison of these sources can be both interesting and informative because of the light it sheds upon the librettist's *modus operandi*: his consideration of the practical aspects of stagecraft, his changing thoughts on the motivations of the characters, and his decisions to alter lines of text and even to add or subtract entire scenes for the sake of dramatic effect. In the discussion of the textual sources, I shall print all of the texts from Rvat that do not appear in Buagni. I shall not print the texts from Buagni found in Rvat, as they will be readily available in my critical edition of *La Statira*.[6]

The edition of Ottoboni's libretto printed by Francesco Buagni contains sixty-eight pages, followed by three unnumbered pages of textual additions. Preceding p. [1] is a view of St. Mark's Square, Venice, from the Bacino; over it hovers a large angel playing a trumpet and holding a banner on which is inscribed the coat of arms of the Ottoboni family. On p. [1] is the title of the work and on p. [2] the imprimatur.

Pp. [3] and [4] contain the dedication.

TO THE LADIES OF ROME

Alexander the Great esteems it more than all of his triumphs to be able to appear in your presence in order to give you in person an entertainment worthy of your interest and of your generosity. He appears on stage first as the lover of Campaspe, then of Statira. He sacrifices the former to his friend

---

[6]W. C. Holmes, ed., *La Statira*, in the series *The Operas of Alessandro Scarlatti*, Donald J. Grout, General Editor (Cambridge, Mass., in press).

and himself to the latter; and he shows you his dilemmas, and to your judgement the motives of his inconstancy, which because they are clothed in glory, can assuredly not displease you. It does you no small honor that the most generous of all the heroes fears your judgement, and aspires to your protection. I am confident, too, that the conqueror of the world will attain even this victory by means of my publication.

> Your Most Humble, Devoted,
> and Obsequious Servant,
>
> Francesco Leone

The *Argomento* follows on pp. [5] and [6]:

Among the most celebrated victories of Alexander is the famous one over himself. He was in love with Campaspe and was having her portrait painted by Apelles, this along with all the other circumstances recounted by Pliny in book 35, chapter x [*sic*; the proper reference is *Naturalis Historia*, book 35, chapter xxxvi]. Seeing that the painter was falling in love with Campaspe, he generously gave her to him.

With this story as the basis, the present drama has been woven. Alexander is waging his third battle against Darius, who is defeated and killed. Statira, the daughter of Darius, is captured with other booty, and Alexander is attracted to her. He is encouraged in his love by Apelles and Demetrius, but earns the displeasure of Campaspe, who, aspiring only to the love of Alexander, looks with hate upon Apelles. Meanwhile, Statira obtains permission from Alexander to retire to a remote place, where her father admonishes her in a dream to return to court and find the consort that heaven wills for her. She does this, and when she declares herself to be the bride of Orontes, the Persian general, Alexander gives his consent so as not to break his word and to the detriment of his own love. Orontes is surprised at the generosity of Alexander and voluntarily withdraws his suit, whereupon (after many incidents) Statira marries Alexander and Campaspe marries Apelles.

The cast of characters appears on p. [7].

MACEDONIANS

Alexander the Great, King of the Macedonians	[soprano]
Campaspe, Alexander's favorite	[soprano]
Apelles, in love with Campaspe	[tenor]
Demetrius, Macedonian general in love with Campaspe	[bass]
Perinto, court servant	[soprano]

PERSIANS

Statira, daughter of Darius, King of Persia, in love with Orontes, later wife of Alexander	[alto]
Orontes, Persian prince, in love with Statira, disguised as Elvio, an Armenian merchant.	[tenor]

DANCES

Of the Persians
Of nymphs

The scene is laid in Damascus.

Finally, on p. [8] are listed the changes of scene.

FIRST ACT

Spacious countryside at night with a moon.
The tent of Darius.
Palace room with statues.
Prison, with remnants of the Persian army, and prisoners sitting upon their shields and destroyed arms.

SECOND ACT

Picture gallery.
Palace room with statues.
Group of mountains with Statira's hut and Darius's mausoleum.

THIRD ACT

Subterranean cavern.

A wood that descends from Statira's hut into a valley.

City square with triumphal arches and royal palace.

Temple of Diana with victims on the altars.

Neither the printed libretto nor any of the extant scores contains a prologue.

The autograph libretto of *La Statira* is in a manuscript volume that appears to be a workbook. The volume contains not only this opera, a great deal of poetry, plot synopses, and literary annotations of various kinds, but also texts to other operas by Ottoboni: *La Forza dell' innocenza* (1690, unfinished), *Amor e gratitudine* (1690), and *Il Colombo* (1690-91). *La Statira* is the first work in the volume; its title page appears on f. 1 and its text concludes on f. 37v, at the bottom of which is written, in Ottoboni's hand, "fine del dramma/ li 4 Marzo/1689."

Ff. 1v, 2, and 2v are blank except for a salutation at the top of f. 2, "Illm:º et Ecc:ᵐº Sig:ʳᵉ mio Col:ᵐº," obviously the beginning of a dedication. At the top of an otherwise blank f. 3 appears the *Argomento*, the garbled and wrongly attributed passage from Pliny mentioned in the printed libretto. F. 3v is blank except for the words "Al Lettore" written at the top, and f. 4 contains the list of characters, including those in the prologue: Pallade, Fortuna, and Tempo. Finally, on f. 4v appear the changes of scene, which differ somewhat from those in the printed libretto.

FIRST ACT

[Prologue] Space. In the middle the globe of the world which is opened into its four parts.

Spacious countryside at night with the moon.

A large tent with a lantern in the middle.

Small garden with a bit of the sea.

Prison where there are the remnants of the Persian army, with prisoners sitting on their shields and destroyed arms.

SECOND ACT

Picture gallery with portraits of Statira and Campaspe.
Salon decorated as the kingdom of Flora, in the apartments of Campaspe.
Group of desolate mountains with the hut of Statira and mausoleum of Darius on the highest one.
Elysian fields with the river Lethe [*sic*] and the boat of Charon to transport souls.

THIRD ACT

Subterranean cavern.
Woods descending from Statira's hut into a valley.
City square with arches [and with intermingled banners with the names of Alexander and Statira] and royal palace.
Temple of Diana with victims on the altars.

The Prologue begins on f. 5. It contains no references to the opera proper, but merely presents the personifications Tempo and Fortuna, seated on elaborate machines, arguing about their respective powers and importance. Tempo begins this discussion with the following lines:

Tempo   Cieca dea, pretendi invano
trionfar del mio poter.
Io sono l'arbitro del mondo . . .

Blind goddess, you try in vain
to triumph over my power.
I am the master of the world . . .

Their argument is interrupted on f. 6 by the entrance of Pallade "on a magnificent group of splendid clouds." Pallade promptly settles the dispute, proclaiming:

Pallade   Cessate le contese . . .
Sia del tempo e della sorte
condottiera la virtù.
D'ambo voi guiderò il piè,

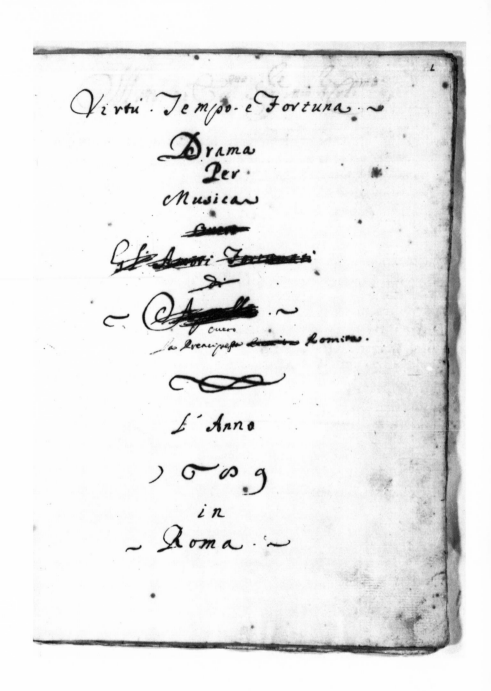

Ill. 3. Title page of the autograph libretto of *La Statira,* finished on March 4, 1689 in Rome (Biblioteca Apolstolica Vaticana, Ottob. Lat. 2360, f.1).

Argomento

Alexander cum dilectam sibi ex *Carissimis* suis precipue Nomine
Campaspen nudam pingi ob admirationem formae ab Apelle
iussisset, eumque tui pari Amore captus sensisset, dono dedit ea
Plin: Naturalis Historia lib: 35 Cap: X: de Artis perpicturam
deaptis. &.

Ill. 4. From the autograph libretto of *La Stàtira,* the *Argomento* quoting a passage from Pliny's *Naturalis Historia* (Biblioteca Apostolica Vaticana, Ottob. Lat. 2360, f. 3).

e mercè
di mie placide ritorte
sia regnar non servitù.
     Sia del etc.

Con prudente consiglio
darò tempo alla sorte e sorte al tempo.
Farò che siano adorni
i giorni da'tesori
e i tesori dai giorni.
Tu, Fortuna, sarai
custodi dei momenti,
ed il Tempo foriero a' tuoi contenti.

Cease these disputes . . .

Virtue is the leader
of time and fate.
I shall guide the movements of both of you,
and the reward
of my quiet restraints
is to be freedom and not servitude.
     Virtue is etc.

With prudent advice,
I shall give time to fate and fate to time.
I shall adorn
the days with treasures
and treasures with long days.
You, Fortune, will be
caretaker of the moments,
and Time the harbinger of your delights.

The three rejoice, and, according to the rubrics, the Prologue ends
with a cortège of the four continents of Europe, Asia, Africa, and
America led around the stage on various animals, amid cries of
"Long live Pallade!"

Before we compare the text as it appears in the autograph and
in the printed libretto, a few words about the sources of Ottoboni's libretto are in order. Statira is the name of the wife as well as

the daughter of Darius, king of Persia. Both are discussed by Plutarch in his *Moralia*, vol. IV, "On the Fortune or the Virtue of Alexander,"[7] and in his *Lives*, vol. VII, "Alexander," chaps. LXX and LXXVII.[8] Ottoboni's *La Statira* incorporates elements from Plutarch and also adds the story of the painter Apelles, found in Pliny. The common bonds between these stories are the life and activities of Alexander the Great. Of the many opera librettos carrying the name of Statira written in the late seventeenth century and the first half of the eighteenth century, Ottoboni's is apparently the only one to follow classical models rather closely.[9]

From Plutarch come those sections dealing with the battle of Issus in 333 B.C., during which Darius was killed; with the capture of Statira; and with Alexander's humane treatment of her and the other Persian prisoners of war. From Pliny Ottoboni extracted the tale of Apelles and Campaspe (Pancaspe in Pliny). Ignoring chronological accuracy, Ottoboni successfully combined these plot lines to make a dramatically coherent libretto with strong delineations of character.

More specifically, the plot of *La Statira* revolves around a number of intrigues that take place after Alexander's defeat of the Persians. Darius is dead, and his daughter, Statira, is taken captive by the Macedonians. Statira, who is betrothed to the Persian prince Orontes, becomes the object of Alexander's affection. But Alexander is loved by Campaspe, who in turn is loved by the court painter Apelles. The jealous Campaspe conspires unsuccessfully to have Statira murdered, enlisting the unwilling aid of the Macedonian general Demetrius, who also loves Campaspe from afar. After

---

[7] Loeb Classical Library edition, pp. 451 ff.

[8] Loeb Classical Library edition, vol. VII, pp. 419 and 437.

[9] The earliest libretto to deal with the story of Statira is by Giovanni Francesco Busenello (music by Cavalli, Venice, 1655). This libretto bears no relationship to the classical accounts. Ottoboni's libretto (1690) is the next known. In 1695 a French tragedy (spoken), *La Statira*, by Nicolas Pradon appeared. The copy of this play found in the Biblioteca Marciana at Venice is from the personal library of Apostolo Zeno. Zeno later collaborated with Pietro Pariati on *La Statira* (music by Francesco Gasparini, Venice, 1705); however, it had little connection with Pradon's tragedy and none whatever with classical models. The *Diario* of Valesio cites performances of Ottoboni's *Statira*, much altered (music by Tomaso Albinoni), at Rome in 1726. (See Cametti, op. cit., p.345.)

many complications, the fabled magnanimity of Alexander provides a happy conclusion to the story—but with a twist. Apelles and Campaspe, who during the course of the opera realize they love one another, are united. Alexander reunites Statira and Orontes, at the same time renouncing his throne and empire in favor of Statira, because of his love for her. Orontes' honor, however, will not allow such a sacrifice on Alexander's part; thus, Orontes withdraws, Statira accepts Alexander's offer of marriage, and all ends happily for the two principal pairs of characters.[10]

[10] For further information on the sources and history of *La Statira*, see my edition of the opera, op. cit.

The Sources Compared

In this section a brief summary of the textual sources will be given and then the differences between them will be analyzed.

ACT I

Scene 1 (Buagni, pp. 9-10; Rvat, f. 7-7v)

Oronte

[Oronte, the Persian general, meditates on the fortunes of battle and his love for Statira.]

The texts agree in both sources.

Scene 2 (Buagni, pp. 10-11; Rvat, ff. 7v-8)

Alessandro, chorus (Oronte also in Rvat)

[Alessandro enters, the battle is fought, and he departs in triumph.]

In the autograph, the Persian army also takes part in the action, and Oronte sings a recitative and aria exhorting his men to defend themselves. His speech, cut in the final version, reads as follows:

19

Oronte   Tempo non è campione
                di quiete o riposo.
                Il nemico orgoglioso,
                con fatali tenzoni,
                vi chiama alle fatiche, e già si sente
                di fremito guerrier l'urto insolente.

                  Ceda il sonno al vostro sdegno.
                  Sù pugnate,
                  conservate
                  con sollecita vittoria
                  vostra gloria;
                  difendete il rege e il regno.
                    Ceda il sonno etc.

Time is no supporter
of quiet and rest.
The proud enemy,
with fatal combat,
calls you to labor, and already one hears
the insolent shout of the trembling warrior.

  Give way your sleep to anger.
  Oh, struggle, maintain your glory
  with prompt victory; defend the king and the king-
    dom.
    Give way etc.

Scene 3 (Buagni, pp. 11-12; lacking in Rvat)

Oronte

[Oronte gives vent to his anguish at having been de-
feated and having lost his beloved Statira.]

Scene 4 (change of scene) (Buagni, pp. 12-13;
Rvat, as Scene 3, ff. 8-8v)

Statira

[Statira mourns over the body of her father,
Dario.]

The text agrees in both sources.

Scene 5 (Buagni, pp. 13-14; Rvat, as Scene 4, ff. 8v-9v.)

Statira, Demetrio, Perinto, Macedonian soldiers

[The Macedonian general Demetrio and the servant Perinto come upon Statira and try to console her.]

Eight lines of the recitative in the autograph are cut from the final version. Ottoboni has marked this cut.

Perinto	Per levarvi dinanzi questo cadaver freddo, fate, signor, venir una lettica con sollecita forma e men fatica.
Demetrio	S'apresti quanto esponi e [illegible] ver Damasco; parti Perinto.
Perinto	Guardo mal voluntiere un corpo estinto.
Perinto	*In order to remove from here* *this cold cadaver* *promptly and with little effort* *sir, call for a litter.*
Demetrio	*Prepare to do what you say,* *and [leave] for Damascus;* *go Perinto.*
Perinto	*I dislike seeing a dead body.*

Scene 5 (Rvat, ff. 9v-10; lacking in Buagni)

Statira, Demetrio

[Statira explains the circumstances of her father's death, and Demetrio suggests that she would be happier were she to leave this place of anguish.]

The text of this scene in the autograph reads as follows:

Statira	Molto ti devo, O prence, e sol mi pesa al desir non conformi aver le forze.
Demetrio	Ma chi Dario svenò?
Statira	Nel sonno immerso udii appena il tumulto, che da barbaro stuolo di vincitrici spade cadde traffitto al suolo.
Demetrio	Questo campo funesto meglio è lasciar; altrove potrai viver più lieta e più sicura.
Statira	Non ha termine ancora la mia sciagura. 　　Mi fidai della speranza 　　ma fallace m'ingannò. 　　Che farò? 　　Chè più m'avanza 　　s'il sperar dalla speranza 　　fu l'error che m'ingannò. 　　Che farò?
Statira	*I owe you much, O prince, and I only am sorry that I have not the means to repay you.*
Demetrio	*But who killed Dario?*
Statira	*I was sound asleep and barely heard the tumult during which he fell to the ground under the victorious swords of the barbarous troops.*
Demetrio	*It would be best for you to leave this baleful place; You will be able to live happier and safer elsewhere.*

Statira   *My plight does not end yet.*

                 I trusted in hope
                 but faithlessly it deceived me.
                 What shall I do?
                 How can I continue
                 if the faith in hope
                 was the error that deceived me?
                 What shall I do?

Scene 6 (Change of scene) (Buagni, p. 15; Rvat, ff. 10-10v)

Campaspe

[Campaspe, Alessandro's mistress, muses on her love and wonders why Alessandro has not visited her since the battle.]

The texts agree in both sources.

Scene 7 (Buagni, p. 6-18; Rvat, ff. 10v-11v)

Campaspe, Apelle, Oronte (disguised as the Armenian, Elvio)

[Oronte is disguised in order to escape capture. Apelle, Alessandro's court painter, listens to Oronte's tale of woe. Oronte wants to find Statira; Apelle hints that Alessandro is attracted to her; Campaspe overhears this and is furious with jealousy.]

In the autograph, Campaspe's closing aria has a second stanza that is cut from the printed libretto:

Campaspe   Non ricuso le catene
                  per chi l'orbe incantenò.
                  Ma che sia
                  l'alma mia
                  d'altri serva, oh questo no!
                    Non ricuso etc.

I do not refuse the chains
with which he [Love] has encircled the globe.
But that
my soul should ever
be the servant of another, oh never this!
I do not refuse etc.

Scene 8 (Buagni, pp. 18-19; Rvat, f. 12)

Apelle, Oronte

[Left with Apelle, Oronte promises to reward him if a meeting can be arranged with Statira.]

The texts agree in both sources.

Scene 9 (Buagni, pp. 20-21; Rvat, ff. 12-12v)

Apelle

[Apelle reflects upon his unrequited love for Campaspe.]

Scene 10 (change of scene) (Buagni, pp. 20-21; Rvat, ff. 12v-13)

Statira, the body of Dario, Persian soldiers in chains

[Statira, in prison, laments her plight, damns her conquerors, and invokes the wrath of the gods.]

Much of the text of Statira's opening recitative is cancelled in the autograph, but, surprisingly, appears in the printed libretto. Brackets indicate cancelled text.

	Rvat	**Buagni**
Statira	[Piombaste] Libraste sovra	Libraste sovra
	il capo de' tiranni . . .	il capo dei tiranni . . .

[Alessandro inumano]	Alessandro inumano
Macedoni inumani . . .	Macedoni inumani . . .
[Chi v'insegnò tiranneggiar gli estinti	
e stringere tra lacci	*[This is printed.]*
chi per fuggir da voi	
l'alma disciolse?]	
Gli dei del cielo invoco	Voi numi eterni invoco
al castigo degl' empii, e	
solo io spero	*[The remainder is*
render col pianto mio	*printed.]*
Giove severo.	

[You pounced upon]	
You counterbalanced	
the leader of the tyrants . . .	
[Inhuman Alessandro]	
Inhuman Macedonians . . .	
[Who taught you to tyran-	
nize the dead and who put	
in chains she who lost her	
soul in fleeing from you?]	
I invoke the gods of	*I invoke you eternal*
heaven to punish the	*gods*
wicked, and I hope, with	
my tears, to make Jove	
angry.	

Statira's closing aria is crossed out and replaced with another text; the new text appears in the printed libretto.

Scene 11 (Buagni, pp. 21-23; Rvat, ff. 13-14)

Statira. Alessandro, Demetrio, Perinto, soldiers in chains

[Alessandro enters, greets Statira, and orders Perinto to release the prisoners. Statira asks that she be allowed to retire as a hermit, and Alessandro reluctantly grants her request.]

Once again, the printed libretto contains some lines that have
been cancelled in the autograph.

	Rvat	**Buagni**
Perinto	. . . [le fredde membra	*[All of the text is*
	ecco di Dario, ed ivi]	*printed.]*
	mira la figlia . . .	
	. . . Here are the cold	
	remains of Dario, and	
	here is his daughter . . .	

Furthermore, the printed libretto contains an aria of two stanzas
for Alessandro that does not appear in the autograph. Only the
first stanza of this aria is set in the scores of the opera.

Alessandro   La clemenza nel cor d'un regnante
è de Febo l'immago verace,
chè non brucia ne fiori, ne piante,
ma le scalda con placida face.
    La clemenza etc.

Regio fiume con pompa quieta
va mordendo le verdi sue sponde,
e se gonfio trapassa le meta
nel suo danno le rende feconde.
    Regio fiume etc.

Clemency in the heart of a monarch
is the true image of Apollo [the sun]
because it does not burn flowers or plants,
but warms them with a placid glow.
    Clemency in etc.

The regal river with quiet pomp
nibbles at its green banks,
and if it overflows its goal,
in its damage it renders the banks fertile.
    The regal river etc.

Following Alessandro's aria in the autograph is an aria for Perinto
that is cut from the final version.

Perinto	Libertà, libertà, consolatevi, da' catene scuotetevi il piè. Rallegratevi, dite uniti viva il re. Libertà etc.
Coro di soldati	Viva il re!
Perinto	*Liberty, liberty, console yourselves, remove your feet from the chains. Rejoice, say together, "Long live the king!" Liberty etc.*
Chorus of soldiers	*Long live the king!*

Scene 12 (Buagni, pp. 23-24; Rvat, f. 14v)

Alessandro, Demetrio, Perinto

*[Demetrio and Perinto suggest to Alessandro that
he take Statira as his wife. Alessandro, without
conviction, refuses.]*

The texts agree in both sources.

Scene 13 (change of scene in Buagni only) (Buagni,
pp. 25-26; Rvat, f. 15)

Demetrio, Perinto, Persian soldiers

*[Demetrio would like Statira to marry Alessandro,
so that Campaspe would then be free for himself.
Perinto suggests that they disguise Elvio, the Armenian (the already disguised Oronte), as a shepherd and send him to plead Alessandro's cause with
Statira.]*

In the autograph, Demetrio sings an aria of two stanzas, the second of which, given here, is cut from the final version.

Demetrio   Voglio, voglio dar pace
             per qualche poco
             a questo cor.
             L'aura che piace
             modera il foco
             del mio dolor.
               Voglio etc.

             I want to give peace
             for a little while
             to this heart.
             The gentle breeze that pleases
             moderates the fire
             of my pain.
               I want to give etc.

Scene 14 (Buagni, p. 26; Rvat, f. 15v.)

Perinto, Persian soldiers

[Perinto exhorts the newly freed prisoners to be happy. There follows a dance of the soldiers.]

In the autograph, two lines of Perinto's recitative are cancelled and replaced. The new lines, however, do not appear in the final version.

Perinto   . . . e con pompa che spiri di gioia e di contento
            date fine al tormento.

            . . . and with magnificence that breathes of joy and
            content make an end to all torment.

ACT II

Scene 1 (Buagni, pp. 27-28; Rvat, ff. 16-16v)

Alessandro, Apelle

[In the picture gallery, Alessandro and Apelle gaze at the portraits of Statira and Campaspe. Alessandro decides that he must have Statira; he then offers Campaspe to Apelle.]

The texts agree in both sources.

Scene 2 (Buagni, pp. 28-30; Rvat, ff. 16v-17)

Alessandro, Apelle, Campaspe

[Campaspe enters and, aware of Alessandro's growing attraction to Statira, tries vainly to extract a pledge of love from him; Apelle then complains of Campaspe's indifference to him.]

The text of Apelle's aria in the printed libretto is garbled in the musical sources:

Buagni	Munich
Esser potrai crudele	Esser potrai crudele
a chi langue per te?	con chi langue per te?
Chè giova esser fedele	Chè giova esser fedele
senza ottener pietà,	senza ottener mercè,
senza sperar mercè?	senza sperar mercè?

London and Cardiff	Modena
Esser potrai crudele	Esser potrai crudele
con chi langue per te?	con chi langue per te?
Chè giova esser fedele	Chè giova esser fedele
senza sperar pietà?	senza sperar mercè?

> Can you be so cruel
> to the one who languishes for you?
> Is it worth being faithful
> without obtaining mercy,
> without hoping for pleasure?

The situation here is further complicated by the fact that the above aria is a substitute and does not appear in the autograph. The aria text in the autograph reads:

Apelle

Veder ch'un'anima
con fede stabile
langue per te,
chè d'amore spasima,
e tu implacabile
negarli fè;
creder questo virtù giusto no è;

> *To see that a soul*
> *with unwavering faith*
> *languishes for you,*
> *that he is deeply in love,*
> *and, implacable you,*
> *to deny him fidelity;*
> *to believe that this is virtuous is not right.*

Scene 3 (Buagni, pp. 30-32; Rvat, ff. 17v-18)

Campaspe, Alessandro, Statira

[Statira enters, thanks Alessandro for his kindnesses to her and to her soldiers, and asks permission to leave for her solitary existence. Alessandro is loathe to let her go, and again Campaspe is consumed with jealousy. Finally, Alessandro agrees to Statira's departure.]

The texts agree in both sources.

Scene 4 (Buagni, pp. 32-33; Rvat, ff. 18-18v)

Campaspe, Statira

*[The women talk about Alessandro's feelings and
Statira assures Campaspe that she need not worry.
Campaspe, however, is not so certain of this.]*

In the autograph, Campaspe's closing aria has two stanzas, only
the first of which is printed in the final version. The text of the
second stanza reads:

Campaspe   Se ben costanti sembrano
                            quei cor che giuran fè,
                            per gioco adorano
                            vaga beltà,
                            e il tosco infiorano
                            di crudeltà.
                            Chè se talor rassembrano
                            d'amar, amor non è.
                              Se ben etc.

                            If those hearts that swear fidelity
                            seem quite constant,
                            they love to dally
                            with rare beauty,
                            and they adorn the poison
                            with cruelty.
                            For if they sometimes seem
                            to love, it is not love.
                              If those hearts etc.

Scene 5 (Buagni, pp. 33-35; Rvat, ff. 19-19v)

Statira, Oronte

*[Oronte enters and is recognized by Statira. He
recounts how he escaped destruction in disguise.
She asks him to steal her portrait in order to re-
move it from Alessandro's sight. Oronte announces*

*that Apelle sent him to plead for Statira to leave
at once so that Campaspe would be free to marry
Alessandro (although Apelle loves her himself).
Statira assures Oronte that she intends to live a
hermit's existence.]*

In the autograph, Statira's closing aria has a second stanza that
was cut from the final version. Its text reads:

Statira   Puro foco mi serpe nel seno
                     il cui raggio m'è caro nel cor.
                     Non ha forza
                     e s'ammorza
                     altra face in sembiante sereno
                     ma in essenza nemica all' onor.
                          Puro foco etc.

*Pure fire crawls in my bosom,
its rays are dear to my heart.
Another fire in a serene visage
does not have force
and is extinguished,
but is essentially the enemy of honor.
     Pure fire etc.*

Scene 6 (Buagni, pp. 35-36; Rvat, f. 20)

Oronte

*[Left alone, Oronte reflects upon his happiness at
seeing Statira once again.]*

In the autograph there is a second stanza to his aria. It is cut
from the final version and reads as follows:

Oronte   Son contento, ancor, ferito
                     e gradito
                     ch'è lo stral che vibra amore;
                     se quel volto
                     che mi tien tra lacci involto
                     mi verrà beato il core.
                          Son contento etc.

> *I am happy, once more*
> *pleasurably wounded*
> *by the darts of love;*
> *my heart becomes happy*
> *by that face*
> *that holds me in its bonds.*
>   *I am happy etc.*

Scene 7 (change of scene) (Buagni, pp. 36-38; Rvat, ff. 20-21v)

Campaspe, Alessandro, Apelle

[Campaspe is discovered in her apartments singing an aria about the powers of love. Alessandro and Apelle enter and remark on her presence and beauty. Apelle muses that Alessandro no longer seems taken with Campaspe, but, when he addresses Campaspe, nevertheless congratulates her on having won Alessandro's affection. Alessandro then announces that he has indeed chosen his bride-to-be, and formally gives Campaspe to Apelle. Both Campaspe and Apelle are taken by surprise. Alessandro sings a final aria and leaves.]

The autograph contains two stanzas for Apelle's aria near the beginning of this scene, but only the second stanza appears in the final version. The text of the first stanza is as follows:

Apelle

> S'ella è vaga e se ti piace,
> perchè fuggi un tanto bel?
> O non hai core
> oppur amore
> cambiò teco la sua face
> e vibrò colpo de gel.
>   S'ella è vaga etc.

> *If she is attractive and if you like her,*
> *why do you flee from such a beauty?*
> *Either you have no heart or love*

> *has changed his torch with you*
> *and let loose a blow of ice.*
> *If she is etc.*

In the autograph, the text of Alessandro's final aria, "Chi a volo troppo alto," is cancelled and replaced by another text. It is the cancelled, original text, however, that appears in the printed libretto.

In this scene the text follows one sequence in the autograph and printed libretto, but quite a different one in the extant scores of the opera. This puzzling situation will be discussed in detail later.

Scene 8 (Buagni, pp. 39-40; Rvat, f. 22)

Campaspe, Apelle

[Campaspe furiously orders Apelle to leave her forever. Apelle declares that he will indeed depart and will kill himself.]

The texts agree in both sources.

Scene 9 (Buagni, pp. 40-41; Rvat, ff. 22v-23)

Campaspe, Demetrio, Perinto

[Demetrio and Perinto enter. Demetrio is surprised to find that Campaspe seems to show him favor. She does so in order to enlist his aid and promises him her love if he will murder both Apelle and Statira. He resolves to do this.]

In the autograph the scene opens with a recitative and aria by Perinto, both of which are cut in the final version.

Perinto   Vel' ho pur detto, ohimè,
                che questa vostra flemma
                non è da innamorato.
                Ecco già terminata
                la pomposa comparsa, e se non sbaglio

il volto di Campaspe
dà segni manifesti di travaglio.
Andate a consolarla,
forse starà così
perchè tardi giungete ad inchinarla.
Andate a consolarla.

Con la femine bisogna
abbondar in diligenza,
caminar speditamente,
e sovente
reputarti a gran vergogna
la più lieve negligenza.
Con la femine etc.

I've already told you, alas,
that this reticence of yours
is not that of one in love.
See, the royal meeting
is already over, and if I am not wrong,
the face of Campaspe
shows definite signs of anxiety.
Go, console her;
perhaps she is thus
because you arrive late to pay your respects.
Go console her.

With women one must
be full of care
go easily,
and often
consider the slightest negligence
a great shame.
With women etc.

In the autograph Campaspe's closing aria has a second stanza
that is cut from the final version.

Campaspe   Offeso mio petto
              t'invio a battaglia.
              Voi larve spietate
              prendete il cor,
              e crude portate
              ruine e terror.
              A placido affetto
              lo sdegno prevale.
                Offeso mio etc.

              My offended breast,
              I send you into battle.
              You merciless spirits,
              take my heart
              and cruelly carry
              ruin and terror.
              Let disdain prevail
              over placid feelings.
                My offended etc.

From this point until the end of Act II, the printed libretto and the autograph display many differences. Following is a summary of these.

	Buagni	Rvat
Scene 10	The text of Demetrio's closing aria is taken from Scene 12 of the autograph	Demetrio's closing aria here is cut from the libretto and substituted.
Scene 11	—	This scene is cut from the libretto.
Scene 12	—	This scene is cut from the libretto. Demetrio's aria here, however, appears in Scene 10 of the libretto.

Scenes 11 and 12 The
text for these scenes is
rearranged from Scene
13 of the autograph.

Scene 13 The text of
this scene is rearranged
in the libretto.

Scene 10 (Buagni, pp. 42-43; Rvat, f. 23v)

Perinto, Demetrio

*[Perinto remarks that love for some women can
lead to disaster. Demetrio, ignoring him, asks fate
to prepare him for the impending murders.]*

In the printed libretto, the text of Demetrio's aria is taken from
Scene 12 of the autograph. Demetrio's original aria as it appears in
Scene 10 of the autograph reads as follows:

Demetrio   Quanto dolce di chi s'ama
                  sia il voler a fido cor.
                  Non lo sa
                  chi di beltà
                  non conobbe lo splendor.
                      Quanto dolce etc.

                  Quanto caro a chi s'adora
                  l'obbedir sempre fu.
                  Dirlo può
                  chi già provò
                  sì gradita servitù.
                      Quanto caro etc.

*How sweet to a faithful heart
is the desire of one who is loved.
He does not know this
who has not enjoyed the splendor
of beauty.
    How sweet etc.*

*How dear obeying has always been
to him who adores.*

He who has already tried
such pleasant servitude
can admit it.
   How dear etc.

Scene 11 (Change of scene) (lacking in Buagni;
Rvat, f. 24)

Oronte

[Oronte, travelling to Statira's hermitage, reflects
on his love for her.]

Oronte   O di sorte incostante
                 sbalzo misero e crudo.
                 Queste, amata Statira,
                 son le tue reggie; Oronte
                 può sol con furti indegni
                 secondar le tue voglie; e a tanto duolo
                 non piangono i macigni, e sordo è il ruolo?
                 Ma non godete, o monti,
                 se celate nel seno
                 donna che per virtù nume si rende.
                 Godete, e le vicende
                 che furo a sì bell'opra il fondamento
                 siano causa dovuta al godimento.

                    Fosco nembo in giorno estivo
                    benchè porti irato il ciglio,
                    pur consola adusto prato.
                    E si vede alzar giulivo
                    qui la rosa e quivi il giglio,
                    l'arso tronco e il curvo lato.
                       Fosco nembo etc.

                    Sembra cruda quella mano
                    che ferisce inferma vena
                    e ne trahe vitale umore.
                    Ma timor di cor insano
                    è il fuggir sì breve pena
                    per soffrir mortal dolore.
                       Sembra cruda etc.

Per alpestre sentiero
verso le care mura
drizzo le piante; o sorte,
quanto fra questi orrori
mi comparti feconda i tuoi tesori.

Oh, I am being thrown about miserably and cruelly
by inconstant fate.
These, beloved Statira,
are your regions; Oronte
can follow your wishes
only with unworthy thefts; do not
the rocks weep and is fate deaf to such pain?
But do not enjoy it, o mountains,
if you conceal within you
a woman who by her virtue is godlike.
Rather, rejoice; the happenings
that were the cause of such a beautiful person
should be the proper reason for rejoicing.

> *Dark cloud on a summer day,*
> *even though you anger the brow,*
> *you nevertheless console the dry field.*
> *And one sees spring up gaily*
> *here the rose and there the lily,*
> *the dry stalk and the curved branch.*
> > *Dark cloud etc.*

> *That hand seems crude*
> *that wounds a weak vein*
> *and takes its vital humors from it.*
> *But the fear of an insane heart*
> *is in fleeing such short unhappiness*
> *in order to suffer mortal pain.*
> > *That hand etc.*

I direct my feet
through mountain guards
toward the beloved walls;
O fate, how much you have compassion on me
with your treasures among these horrors.

Scene 12 (lacking in Buagni; Rvat, f. 24v)

Demetrio

[Demetrio, disguised as a shepherd, prepares himself to carry out the murders.]

In the printed libretto, Demetrio's opening aria in this scene becomes a substitute for his aria in Scene 10. The recitative following the aria does not appear in the printed libretto.

Demetrio	A voi dimando il cor,
	belve più fiere,
	insegnatemi,
	mostratemi
	il velen
	che celate in sen;
	se per seguir amor
	armarsi di furor
	deve il pensiere.
	A voi etc.

Ho da svenar Statira,
Apelle a consacrar all'idol mio.
Onde voi scielgo, o monti,
per are al sacrificio, ed a me sia
foco il sol, tempio il bosco, e conche i fonti.

> *My heart asks of you,*
> *wild beasts,*
> *teach me,*
> *show me*
> *the poison*
> *that you conceal in your breasts;*
> *for in order to follow love*
> *the mind must*
> *arm itself with fury.*
>   *My heart etc.*

I must kill Statira,
and sacrifice Apelle to my beloved.

Therefore, I choose you, O mountains,
to be altars for the sacrifice and, for me,
let the sun be the fire, the forest be the temple,
and the streams be the conchshell.

Scene 11 (Change of scene) (Buagni, pp. 43-44; Rvat, the first part of Scene 13, ff. 24v-25)

Statira

[Statira in her hermitage sings of her longing to join her dead father. She gradually falls asleep.]

In the autograph, Demetrio enters and sings four lines of recitative that are cut from the printed libretto.

Demetrio	Eccola appunto arride
	A' miei disegni il fato.
	Sù, coraggio all'impresa;
	destati, o crudeltà.

There she is; fate
helps me in my plans.
Take courage for this deed;
awaken, O cruelty.

Scene 12 (Buagni, pp. 44-45; Rvat, the last part of Scene 13, ff. 25-25v)

Demetrio, Statira

[As Statira sleeps, dreaming and talking of her father, Demetrio approaches. Before he can stab her, a huge earthquake begins, and he flees in terror.]

In the printed libretto, this scene opens with the lines of Demetrio's recitative, cut in the preceding scene. The recitative continues, but omits two lines from the autograph.

Demetrio	O ciel, quando son giunto a compir l'opra. . . ?

O heaven, when shall I be able
to complete the deed. . . ?

ACT III

Scene 1 (Buagni, p. 46; lacking in Rvat)

Alessandro

[In this added scene, Alessandro sings two arias and a recitative about the problems of a lover. In his own mind he is not at all certain which of the two ladies he loves.]

Scene 2 (Buagni, p. 47; Rvat, as Scene 1, f. 26)

Apelle

[Apelle sings of his hopeless position with regard to Campaspe. He is about to commit suicide.]

The texts agree in both sources.

Scene 3 (Buagni, pp. 48-49; Rvat, as Scene 2, ff. 26-26v)

Oronte, Apelle

[Oronte rushes in and prevents the suicide. As he and Apelle argue, they hear a woman's voice off stage screaming for help.]

The texts agree in both sources.

Scene 4 (Buagni, pp. 49-51; Rvat, as Scene 3, ff. 26v-27)

Campaspe, Apelle, Oronte

[Campaspe appears, pursued by a lion. Apelle and Oronte kill the beast. In the ensuing conversation, Campaspe begs forgiveness for having ordered the murders. She learns that it was Oronte and not Apelle who stole Statira's portrait, and she realizes that she does indeed love Apelle.]

In the autograph the scene opens with a recitative that is cut from the printed libretto.

Campaspe	Amici, a voi sol tocca levarmi dal periglio.
Oronte **Apelle**	Non temo, no, mostro crudel l'artiglio.
Campaspe	Apelle, qui?
Oronte **Apelle**	Resisti invan, sei vinto, e l'errore commesso la tua morte compensa.

Uccidono il leone.

Campaspe	*Friends, it is up to you* *to take me from danger.*
Oronte **Apelle**	*I do not fear the monster's claws.*
Campaspe	*Apelle here?*
Oronte **Apelle**	*You resist in vain,* *and the error you committed* *will bring your death.*

They kill the lion.

In the printed libretto, the first stanza of the closing aria is assigned to Oronte and the second stanza to Campaspe. In the autograph, Oronte sings both stanzas.

> *Scene 5* (Buagni, pp. 51-52, with added text on the
> unnumbered pages following p. 68 of the libretto;
> Rvat, as Scene 4, without the added text, f. 28)
>
> **Campaspe, Apelle**
>
> *[This is a love scene for Campaspe and Apelle.]*

With the exception of the added text in the printed libretto, the
sources agree.

> *Scene 6* (change of scene) (Buagni, pp. 52-53;
> Rvat, as Scene 5, ff. 28-28v)
>
> **Perinto, soldiers**
>
> *[Perinto, wending his way toward Statira's hermit-
> age, muses on her unhappiness, on Demetrio's
> treacherous plans, and on the futility of being a
> lover.]*

The texts agree in both sources.

> *Scene 7* (Buagni, pp. 53-54; Rvat, as Scene 6, ff.
> 28v-29)
>
> **Statira, Oronte, Perinto, soldiers**
>
> *[Oronte tells Statira of Campaspe's confession; he
> does not know who tried to kill Statira. Statira
> seeks no revenge. Perinto and the soldiers arrive;
> they have been sent to guard Statira. Grateful, Sta-
> tira orders Perinto to tell Alessandro she wishes to
> to see him.]*

The autograph contains a closing aria for Perinto that has been
cancelled.

The texts agree in both sources.

Scene 8 (Buagni, pp. 54-56; Rvat, as Scene 7, ff. 29-30)

Statira, Oronte, later Demetrio

[Statira and Oronte continue their discussion of the attempted murder. Demetrio enters and confesses his role in it. He was prevented from completing the act by the heavens and earth, which erupted into a storm and an earthquake. Statira immediately pardons him and sings that the best revenge is kindness.]

In the autograph, after Demetrio's confession, Statira in a long monologue describes what happened to her at the time of the attempted murder. This monologue is cut from the printed libretto.

Statira	Udite, amici, udite
	con stupor la mia voce. In quel momento
	che Demetrio tentava
	darmi un'ingiusta morte, in sogno viddi
	Pluton, re dell'inferno, il qual mi disse:
	Donna, se il padre estinto
	brami veder io son contento; lieta
	ricevei la proposta. Allor distese
	vasto dragon i vanni all'aria bruna
	e fattosi di me soma sul dorso,
	con brevissimo corso
	mi portò negl'elisi ove conobbi
	tra mille alme beate il genitore.
	Mi consolò, mi strinse
	dolcemente la destra, e poi mi disse:
	Lascia l'eremo, o figlia,
	lascia di pianger più; vanne alla corte
	ove nobil consorte
	con puro ardor discaccierà dal core
	queste funeste larve;
	lo vuol il ciel. Ed in ciò disparve.
Oronte	Che vuoi di più se il fato
	con note così chiare
	ti vuol felice?

Demetrio   Appunto.
T'udii nel sonno proferire Averno,
mostri, larve, Plutone, e quanto ascolto
confermo dal passato.

Statira   *Listen, friends, listen*
to my voice with wonder. In that moment
that Demetrio tried
to cause my unjust death, in a dream I saw
Pluto, king of the underworld, who said to me:
"Woman, if you want to see your dead
father, I am agreeable"; happily
I received the news. Then a huge dragon
extended his wings in the smoky air,
and I mounted him;
in a very short journey,
he carried me to the Elysian Fields, where I saw,
among a thousand blessed souls, my father.
He consoled me, and took me
gently by the hand, saying:
"Leave the hermitage, O daughter,
do not weep anymore; go to the court
where a noble consort
with great ardor will throw from your heart
these dark spirits;
heaven wills it." And with that he disappeared.

Oronte   *What more do you wish if fate*
with such clear signs
wants you happy?

Demetrio   *Exactly.*
I heard you in your sleep mention the underworld,
spirits, Pluto, monsters; what I hear now
I confirm from the past.

Aside from this passage, the texts agree in both sources.

Scene 9 (change of scene) (Buagni, pp. 56-58; Rvat, as Scene 8, ff. 30v-31)

Alessandro, Apelle

[Alessandro and Apelle plan a double wedding. Apelle suggests that the rites be performed at the temple, where all the trappings of ceremony will induce Statira to accept Alessandro's proposal.]

In the printed libretti, near the beginning of the scene, Alessandro has an aria of two stanzas. This text does not appear in complete form in the autograph. The first line, however, is scribbled in the margin of the autograph beside some cancelled lines of recitative, which indicates that the aria was meant to be added.

Scene 10 (Buagni, p. 58; Rvat, as Scene 9, f. 31)

Alessandro, Perinto

[Perinto announces the imminent arrival of Statira, and Alessandro directs him to take her to the temple.]

In the autograph, Alessandro's closing aria has two stanzas, the second of which, given here, was cut from the printed libretto.

Alessandro   Se quel sol l'amato oggetto
dal mio cor voti riceve,
che esaudisca in sacro tetto
le mie preci ben si deve.
     Se quel sol etc.

If that sun, the beloved object,
receives vows from my heart,
then let her answer
my prayers under a sacred roof.
     If that sun etc.

Scene 11 (Buagni, pp. 59-60; Rvat, as Scene 10,
ff. 31v-32)

Perinto, Campaspe

*[Perinto taunts Campaspe, but she maintains that
she loves only Apelle and has no interest in Demetrio. They prepare to depart for the temple, and
Campaspe asks to be allowed to beg forgiveness
from Statira. Perinto assures her that Statira will
show compassion.]*

In the autograph, but not in the libretto, the scene closes with
a recitative and aria by Perinto.

Perinto	Così varia d'aspetto
	chi prattica la corte
	ed acconcia il suo petto
	ai duri cangiamenti della sorte.
	Costei quando credea
	d'esser dal re gradita,
	rivale di Statira dicea,
	e con speranza ardita
	se l'offese tentò. Cerca il perdono
	or che la vede approsimata al trono.
	Imparate cortigiano
	questa logica importante:
	sia che va prospero il vento
	concludete l'argomento,
	perché può d'oggi in dimani
	cambiar scuola il cattedrante.
	Imparate etc.

*Thus one who plays the courtier
and prepares herself
for the unpleasant quirks of fate
changes her point of view.
When she believed
she was the king's favorite,*

she said Statira was her rival
and, with bold hope,
tried to harm her. Now that
she sees Statira near the throne,
she seeks pardon.

Courtiers, learn
this important lesson:
unless the wind is blowing in your favor,
finish the argument;
because, between today and tomorrow, it is
possible for the professor to change schools.
Courtiers, learn etc.

Scene 12 (Buagni, pp. 60-61; Rvat, as Scene 11, ff. 32-32v)

Oronte, Statira, Perinto, Campaspe

[Statira arrives with Oronte. She is told that Alessandro awaits her in the temple. Campaspe approaches and asks forgiveness, which is granted. Statira's final aria consoles Oronte for his many trials.]

In the autograph, this aria has two stanzas, the second of which is cut in the libretto. The omitted text is as follows:

Statira Dei tuoi sospiri
ascolta il suono
quest'alma mia.
I tuoi desiri
con egual dono
saziar desia.
    Dei tuoi etc.
My soul
listens to the sound
of your sighs.
It wants to satisfy
your desires
with the same largesse.
    My soul etc.

Scene 13 (Change of scene in autograph) (Buagni,
p. 62; Rvat, as Scene 12, f. 33)

Demetrio

*[In the temple alone, Demetrio sings that he no
longer wants anything to do with love.]*

The autograph contains a second stanza to this aria that is cut
from the libretto.

Demetrio   Dea dei boschi, il sciolto core
                   vò che solo sia di te.
                   Tu m'assisti e fa che amore
                   lungi voli pur da me.
                       Dea dei boschi etc.

                   Goddess of the forests, I want
                   my freed heart to be yours only.
                   Help me and let love
                   fly away from me.
                       Goddess etc.

Scene 14 (Buagni, pp. 62-63; Rvat, as the opening
of Scene 13, f. 33)

Apelle, Demetrio, Perinto, Alessandro

*[Awaiting the arrival of Statira, Alessandro is not
certain she will accept his proposal. Perinto, in an
aside, allows that she may love someone else, but
Apelle is certain that all will turn out well.]*

The texts agree in both sources.

Scene 15 (Buagni, pp. 63-66; Rvat, as the remainder of Scene 13, ff. 33v-34v)

**Statira, Oronte, Alessandro, Demetrio, Apelle,
Perinto**

*[Statira enters and tells Alessandro how in a dream
her dead father exhorted her to go to court and*

*find a noble consort. Alessandro, of course, agrees
to this. Statira then stupefies those assembled by
announcing that she will marry Oronte and explains that he is the disguised Persian prince who
loves her. Alessandro hands her a document which
he says contains his reaction to this announcement
and abruptly turns to leave.*

The texts agree in both sources.

Scene 16 (Buagni, pp. 66-68 and the additional
text on unnumbered pages following p. 68; Rvat,
as Scene 14, without the added text, ff. 35-37v)

**Alessandro, Statira, Oronte, Apelle, Demetrio
Perinto, Campaspe**

*[Campaspe rushes on stage to prevent Alessandro
from leaving; he announces that he has given up
Statira to Oronte, and that he has renounced his
crown in her favor. Statira reads his note confirm-
ing this information. Oronte, confused, declares
that he cannot be the cause of such a sacrifice and
withdraws his claim on Statira. Alessandro asks
Statira to marry him and she accepts. Campaspe
sings a joyful aria, then the goddess Diana appears
on a mechanized cloud and blesses the two pairs
of lovers—Alessandro and Statira, and Apelle and
Campaspe. The opera ends with Alessandro and
Apelle each singing one stanza of a two-stanza aria.*

At the bottom of f. 37v in the autograph, Ottoboni has written:
"Fine del dramma/ li 2 Marzo/ 1689." Thus the first version of the
text of *La Statira* was completed when Ottoboni was 22 years old,
more than five months before the death of Innocent XI and more
than eight months before Ottoboni's granduncle ascended the
papal throne as Alexander VIII.

Not surprisingly, there are many differences between the autograph and the printed libretto throughout the opera; also not surprisingly, the autograph is longer than the final version that was

printed and set to music. To begin at the end, there are three versions of the opera's last scene: one in the printed libretto and two in the autograph manuscript. Two of these are summarized in the following table, and the third will be described in the ensuing discussion.

Buagni	Rvat
Recit., p. 66	Recit., f. 35
Recit., p. 67	Recit., f. 35
Recit., p. 67	Recit., f. 36v (top)
Recit., p. 68	Recit., f. 37 (top)
Aria (Campaspe), p. 68	Aria (Campaspe), f. 37 (middle)
Aria (Diana) added text	—
Recit. (Diana) added text	—
Aria (Diana) added text	—
Recit., p. 68	Recit., f. 36v (bottom)
Aria (Apelle and Alessandro), p. 68	Aria (Apelle and Alessandro), f. 36v (bottom)

In the autograph, the text is muddled and confused, with many changes and cancellations. On f. 35 of the autograph the recitative begins as it does on pp. 66-67 of the printed libretto. At the bottom of this page, however, Ottoboni directs the reader to the top of f. 36v, where there appear eight lines of text that form a continuation of the preceding recitative. Near the middle of f. 36v there is another indication to proceed to the top of f. 37, where this lengthy recitative concludes. The text of Campaspe's aria follows. At the end of this aria, the reader is directed back to the middle of f. 36v for the recitative that comes next. There is no indication of Diana's appearance here. The recitative is followed by the text of the final aria, sung by Alessandro and Apelle. The many cancellations represent slightly different versions of the final printed text (minus the added text for Diana): the cancelled text on f. 35v is a longer version of the recitative on f. 36v, and the cancelled aria at the bottom of f. 35v is recopied on f. 36v with slight changes. There is one blank page, f. 36.

At the bottom of f. 36v, an alternate ending to the opera is given, introduced as follows:

> and it is possible to end the
> drama in the following manner.

The cancelled text for this alternate ending appears on ff. 37-37v.

f. 37

Alessandro   Svenate, olà, della gola la fiera,
a rimbombi festiva
la voce d'ogni cor.

Popolo   Diana viva.

f. 37v

*Salito Alessandro e Statira in trono preparatogli,
il sacerdote maggiore svena la vittima e la
consuma col fuoco, mentre li quattro cori
cantano in falsobordone il seguente*

MADRIGALE

O virtù, quanto puoi
nel petto degli'eroi
se con nodo tenace
il Tempo e la Fortuna unisci in pace.
E fai che a lor desiri
servan numi fecondi di martiri,
onde chi vuol gioir segua virtute
chè in lei si trova sol ver salute.

[*In the margin*: dovrà esservi il maestro di capella
come all'uso moderno che faccia la battuta]

Alessandro   *Cut, then, the beast's throat
and let everyone's voice
ring out festively.*

Populace   *Long live Diana.*

> *Once Alessandro and Statira have ascended the*
> *throne prepared for them, the high priest kills the*
> *sacrificial victim and burns it, while the four*
> *choruses sing, in falsobordone style, the following,*

MADRIGAL

> *O Virtue, unite with*
> *a firm knot, as best you can,*
> *Time and Fortune within the*
> *breasts of heroes in peace.*
> *And let gods full of torments*
> *serve their desires;*
> *thus he who wants happiness should*
> *   follow Virtue,*
> *because one finds pure well-being*
> *   only in Her.*

[*In the margin*: there should be a conducter in the
modern way, giving the beat]

The text of this closing "madrigal" recalls the original title of
opera– *Virtú, Tempo, e Fortuna.*

Three complete scenes appearing in the autograph are cut from
the printed libretto: Act I, Scene 5; Act II, Scene 11; and Act II,
Scene 12. (However, Demetrio's aria from Act II, Scene 12 in the
autograph is transferred to Act II, Scene 10 in the libretto, and re-
places for the original aria in that scene.) Ottoboni put a large "X"
in the left margin of the autograph at the beginning of Act I,
Scene 5; this was his usual mark to signify a change. From a
dramatic point of view, this scene adds little to what we already
know, and therefore could be dispensed with. Statira had previous-
ly been introduced into the plot, and her situation made known.
The scene following this discarded scene in the printed libretto
introduces another major character, Campaspe. On the other hand,
the discarded Scene 5 of the autograph attempts, for the first time
in the opera, to explain the circumstances of King Dario's death.
Furthermore, in this scene it is the Macedonian general, Demetrio,

who suggests to Statira that she would be safer and happier were she to leave Alessandro's court. This is in contrast to the final version of the opera, where, later in Act I it is Statira herself who asks Alessandro to allow her to leave and live in solitude.

Tightening up the end of Act II by eliminating Scenes 11 and 12, makes a great deal of sense dramatically. By this point in the action, Alessandro has displayed his ambivalent feelings towards Statira; Campaspe has rejected Apelle's suit and, consumed with jealousy, has urged Demetrio to murder Statira and Apelle. In Act II, Scene 10, Demetrio prepares himself emotionally to commit the murders. In the autograph, Scene 11 is for Oronte alone and does nothing to further the action. Indeed, this scene interrupts the rapid flow of events that conclude Act II and was sensibly omitted. In Scene 12 Demetrio essentially repeats the actions in Scene 10. The scenes are so similar that, in the final version, Demetrio's aria in Scene 12 of the autograph can replace his autograph aria in Scene 10 without seeming out of place.

The printed libretto, then, jumps from Demetrio's musing in Scene 10 of the auograph to the final scenes of the act, in which he attempts to murder Statira as she sleeps, but is foiled by the elements. These Scenes 11 and 12 in the printed libretto are made up of texts slightly rearranged from Scene 13 of the autograph. As Demetrio raises his dagger over Statira, a violent storm and earthquake erupt. He flees and the act ends. The autograph contains extensive stage directions that do not appear in the libretto. According to these directions, the rock upon which Statira is sleeping suddenly becomes a winged dragon that carries her into the air without awakening her. As Demetrio flees, the earth opens to reveal the river Lethe (*sic*), with Charon transporting the souls of the dead. Some of the souls arise on a cloud to console Statira, while others dance below. All then vanishes as suddenly as it had appeared. Even without this elaborate apparatus, there must have been a great deal of music added at the end of the act. Certainly, a complicated dream sequence and an earthquake require more than merely the recitative found in the scores.

Two complete scenes appear in the printed libretto that have no counterparts in the autograph. These are of special interest, for, as will be discussed later, they raise the important probability that the music for these scenes was composed not by Scarlatti, but by a different composer.

Act I, Scene 3 is the first of these, and completes what can be described as an extended dramatic unit. The first three scenes of Act I form a compact segment that runs the gamut of emotional intensity. First comes a scene of quiet reflection by Oronte alone, on the eve of the battle. This is followed by the battle scene itself. It will be recalled that this scene is much more elaborate in the autograph than in the final printed version, where Oronte's recitative and aria are cut. From a practical point of view, it would have been very difficult to follow Ottoboni's original intentions in performance. The entrance of opposing armies, interruption of the action with a recitative and aria by Oronte, the extended battle itself, and the number of supernumeraries required for such a scene not only would have slowed the dramatic action, but also would have involved considerable expense. The final version of the scene still presents staging problems, but they are not insurmountable. Next is Scene 3, another solo scene for Oronte. This extraordinary scene is singled out for special musical treatment. Beginning with the words, "Crudo ciel, empio fato," it is an extended accompanied recitative whose internal organization raises parts of it to the threshold of true aria. The musical organization of this scene can be described as follows: ritornello A; accompanied recitative with an internal organization of *aba*; ritornello B; accompanied recitative containing elements of ritornello B; accompanied recitative (marked "adagio"); ritornello A. This organization, reflecting the various changes of mood in the text, is the most sophisticated in the entire opera.

The other complete scene found in the printed libretto but not in the autograph is Act III, Scene 1, for Alessandro alone. This scene, consisting of an aria, a recitative, and a second aria, affords Alessandro yet another occasion to display his confused emotions toward Statira and Campaspe, although twice before (in Act II, Scene 1 and in Act II, Scene 7) he had publicly announced that he intended to take Statira as his wife and give Campaspe to Apelle. Perhaps Ottoboni did not write the text for this scene, for it fails to take into account the earlier announcements in the libretto concerning Alessandro's intentions. Analogies can be drawn between Alessandro's scene in Act III and Oronte's in Act I: both afford a principal singer an additional solo scene in which he can display his vocal powers; both appear only in the printed libretto; and, finally, the music for Oronte's entire scene and for one aria of Alessandro's scene appear elsewhere ascribed to a composer other than Scarlatti.

One other complete scene warrants discussion, although it appears in both the autograph and the printed libretto: this is Act II, Scene 7. As mentioned earlier, this scene is remarkable in a number of ways. Aside from the battle scene (Act I, Scene 2) and the final scene of the opera, it calls for the most elaborate stage machinery in the entire work. The stage directions in the autograph, which appear in the musical scores but not in the printed libretto, read as follows:

> *A large room in Campaspe's apartments*
> *with a huge float of flowers in the*
> *middle, and everything decorated to*
> *resemble the kingdom of Flora. Campaspe*
> *seated upon the float, which is drawn*
> *by two white chargers, dressed as*
> *Flora, surrounded by many maidens repre-*
> *senting the most notable flowers of the*
> *world. In the air, a number of little*
> *cupids who together scatter*
> *flowers on the stage.*

After the first sentence in the autograph, Ottoboni inserted three lines of text for Perinto, but cancelled them and continued as above.

In this scene, as in one other in the opera, there are fundamental differences between the two groups of sources. The ordering of the text in the autograph is identical with that in the printed libretto, but the musical sources all agree on an ordering that is quite different. In the textual sources, Campaspe is discovered a alone surrounded by the mass of machinery. As described earlier, she sings an aria about the power of love; this is followed by a short recitative in which she calls upon Alessandro, her lover, to return to her arms. Alessandro and Apelle enter and sing a short recitative; then follows Apelle's aria reminding Alessandro how much Campaspe loves him. The two notice Campaspe. Apelle tells her that she has won Alessandro from her rival, Statira, and Campaspe berates Alessandro for his seeming unfaithfulness. She then sings an aria in which she expresses the wish to punish him. In the succeeding recitative, Alessandro finally informs Campaspe and Apelle—to their utter astonishment—that he has no intention of taking Campaspe as his wife and that he is giving her to Apelle, who has always loved her. In an aria, Alessandro then warns Campaspe that she has set her sights too high.

In the scores, the scene begins differently. Alessandro and Apelle enter speaking of Campaspe, and Apelle sings his aria. It is only after this that Campaspe sings the aria that opens the scene in the textual sources. The short recitative follows in which she calls for Alessandro's return, and Apelle announces to her—also in recitative—that she has indeed won Alessandro's affection. The scene then continues and concludes as it does in the autograph and printed libretto.

A plausible explanation for these differences suggests itself if we examine aspects of both dramatic pacing and practical stagecraft. Until this point, Act II has had no change of scene; all of the action has taken place in the royal picture gallery. Now the scene is shifted to the very elaborately decorated apartments of Campaspe—a change that would take some time to effect. Statira and Oronte appeared in Scene 5, and Oronte was alone in Scene 6, immediately preceding this one. It makes dramatic and practical sense for Alessandro and Oronte to appear in the picture gallery setting, rather than in Campaspe's apartments in her presence, to discuss Alessandro's relationship with her. The audience would then be prepared for the ensuing scene in which Campaspe takes part. It is precisely such a solution that appears in two of the musical sources. Both the Cardiff and Modena scores split Scene 7 into two scenes, labeled Scenes 7 and 8. It is only after the discussion between Alessandro and Apelle, including Apelle's aria, that the lengthy scenic description appears, at the beginning of the newly created Scene 8. Whoever made the changes in the musical sources, whether the original scene was divided into two parts or not, merely transposed the conversation between Alessandro and Apelle from its position following Campaspe's aria in the autograph and printed libretto to a position immediately preceding her aria. Both the Munich and London scores, on the other hand, while they also present the text in this order, give the scenic description before the conversation and do not divide Scene 7. Perhaps this version implies that, though the sets were changed earlier, Campaspe did not make her entrance on the float until after Apelle's aria. Whatever the case, the ordering of the text in the scores is certainly preferable to that in the autograph and printed libretto, in which, after her aria, Campaspe would have to sit (unnoticed) while Alessandro and Apelle talk about her.

It is clear from one musical source that the problematical aspects of the original text were recognized while the manuscript was being copied, and the changes were made at that time. The copyist of the Munich manuscript—the source closest to the earliest performances of *La Statira*—apparently became confused at one point in Scene 7 and left us ample evidence of this confusion. In the textual reordering found in the musical sources, Campaspe's first recitative—which in the autograph is interrupted by the appearance of Alessandro and Apelle—is joined to the later, long recitative sung by all three of the characters. The Munich copyist made a mistake at the point in the recitative (between measures 9 and 10) where the autograph originally contained a break for the entrance of Alessandro and Apelle. He began to copy the text and music in the origianl ordering, a fact which indicates that Scarlatti probably had composed his music according to the sequence of the text in the autograph. The copyist then realized that changes were to be made, crossed out a measure, forgot to complete the cadence of Campaspe's recitative, and continued copying the new, combined version. The copyists of the scores at London, Cardiff, and Modena, however, added a measure at this point—a whole note in the continuo—to complete a cadence in A minor and thus make a proper, if awkward, close (the next segment of recitative begins in B minor). Apparently, by the time these later scores were copied what had begun as an alteration had become standardized.

In the printed libretto, there are extensive textual additions to Act III on unnumbered pages following the main body of the text. Act III, Scene 5—an otherwise unremarkable love scene between Campaspe and Apelle—is greatly expanded by these additions. In the autograph and in the body of the printed libretto, the scene opens with a recitative followed by a two-stanza aria, the first stanza of which is sung by Campaspe, and the second by Apelle. It is at this point that the new text is added, dividing the two stanzas of the aria. These additions alter the dramatic situation considerably. Campaspe sings the first stanza protesting her love for Apelle. Apelle answers with an arietta (added), declaring that he really should die because he cannot bear to lose her again. In the following short recitative (added), Campaspe reassures him, and he appears convinced. He then sings the second stanza of the aria. The lovers' problems are not yet completely resolved, however. In a recitative (added), Campaspe chides Apelle for his lack of trust in her and threatens to leave. He consoles her, and they close the scene with a short duet (added). Thus, the added texts—the purpose of which is to delay the final, mutual declarations of love—increase the dramatic impact of an otherwise quite conventional scene. Furthermore, a textual and dramatic parallelism is established which manages to balance the changing feelings of both of the lovers:

1. Campaspe sings of her love (stanza 1)
2. Apelle doubts her (arietta)
3. Campaspe reassures him (recitative)
4. Apelle is convinced (stanza 2)
5. Campaspe, however, must have her turn to doubt (recitative)
6. Finally, all doubts are resolved (duet)

In the printed libretto, the added texts (nos. 2, 3, 5, 6) are incorrectly labeled "Atto II, Scena quinta."

The other added text in Act III is found in the closing scene of the opera and has nothing to do with the drama proper. It merely allows for the appearance of the goddess Diana supported by elaborate machinery. As the stage directions read: "Diana on a cloud surrounded by many little cupids." Diana sings two short arias separated by a recitative and departs as the story comes to its happy conclusion. As discussed earlier, the London score alone follows the autograph and omits this appearance of Diana.

There are two other textual additions, not labelled as such, which both appear in the body of the printed libretto: Alessandro's arias in Act I, Scene 11 and in Act III, Scene 9. The first of these contains two printed stanzas, although only the first stanza is set to music in any of the extant complete scores. This text is clearly a quite late insertion, for there is no mention of an aria at this point in the autograph. It is a different matter with the aria added in Act III, Scene 9. Its complete text does not appear in the autograph; but in the right-hand margin, beside a few lines of cancelled recitative, Ottoboni wrote out the first lines of the aria text, "Dai colpi d'un guardo, sol nasce . . .," followed by a large asterisk. The text that appears in the printed libretto, therefore, was obviously meant by the librettist to be included.

A number of complete arias as well as stanzas from arias that appear in the autograph have been cut from the printed libretto. The one character who suffers most from these deletions is, not surprisingly, Perinto, the servant. In the autograph Perinto is given four arias in Act I, one in Act II, and two in Act III. In the libretto, however, he has only four arias altogether: three in Act I and one in Act III.

In addition, three autograph arias for other characters are cut from the printed libretto. Two are near the end of Act II: Demetrio's aria from Act II, Scene 10, and Oronte's aria from Act II, Scene 11—a scene that, it will be recalled, was deleted completely from the final version of the opera. These cuts are the result of Ottoboni's extensive rearrangement of the closing scenes of Act II.

The third omitted aria is a special case and represents the sole instance in the opera where an autograph text is substituted by another text in the printed libretto. In Act II, Scene 2, Apelle's autograph aria, "Veder ch'un'anima" is replaced by another aria, beginning "Esser potrai crudele." In the autograph, a mark appears in the left-hand margin that could be interpreted as a sign to replace the aria, although it is not the usual symbol employed by Ottoboni to indicate such substitutions. As mentioned earlier, it is the text "Esser potrai crudele" that appears in garbled versions in the various scores.

One long, important recitative appearing in the autograph was

cut from the printed libretto—and for good reason. In the autograph, the text of Statira's long monologue in Act III, Scene 8 de-
scribing in detail her father's appearance to her in a dream is re-
peated verbatim in Act III, Scene 15. In the printed libretto, however, the monologue appears only in Scene 15 and has been
omitted from Scene 8. Apparently, it was decided that one such
monologue was enough.

The omission in the printed libretto of stanzas appearing in the
autograph is a common enough phenomenon and normally would
be mentioned only in passing. It is worth noting, however, that
some of the missing autograph stanzas are in fact set in one or
another of the complete scores. The second stanza of Campaspe's
aria in Act I, Scene 7 and Demetrio's aria in Act I, Scene 13 are
both set in the Cardiff manuscript; and the second stanza of Campaspe's aria in Act II, Scene 4 appears in the London score. It
would seem, then, that the copyists of the scores at Cardiff and
London had access to the autograph libretto.

More importantly, there are many texts, stanzas from arias, and
complete arias appearing in the autograph that are contained neither in the printed libretto nor in the scores, but are found set to
music in another source—a collection of arias from *La Statira* at
the Conservatory of San Pietro a Majella in Naples, Ms. 34.5. 13
(INc). The volume is in typical oblong format with the date 1693
appearing on its first page and again on its final page, f. 118. The
collection opens with an *Aria con quattro violini* and closes with a
cantata entitled *Il Leandro*. Between these two works appear a
number of arias from *La Statira*. Unlike many aria collections of
the time, some of the arias here are copied with orchestral ac-
companiment. In fact, the copyist grouped the arias with orchestra
separately from those accompanied only by the continuo.

Before listing the complete arias and single stanzas found set to
music only in this collection, let us consider some of the texts that
do *not* appear here. First, none of the texts that are absent from
the autograph but were added to the body or at the end of the
printed libretto is found here.(Act I, Scene 3; Act I, Scene 11; Act
II, Scene 2; Act III, Scene 1; Act III, Scene 5; Act III, Scene 9;
Act III, Scene 16). Second, only one of the texts appearing in a
Roman manuscript to be discussed a little later is found here. This

one text, however, is set to different music in INc. Finally, none
of Perinto's arias appears in the Naples manuscript. As for the remainder of the texts not found in INc, there seems to be no pat-
tern governing their omission.

The texts that appear in INc but not in the complete scores of
the opera can be divided into three distinct groups:

1) Aria texts found in the autograph scenes that were omitted
entirely from the printed libretto (Statira's aria in Act I, Scene 5;
Oronte's aria in Act II, Scene 11). Demetrio's aria in Act II, Scene
10 of the autograph can also be included in this group, for in the
libretto and the scores it is replaced by the aria for Demetrio originally appearing in Act II, Scene 12, which was cut from the
printed libretto.

2) Aria texts, either first or second stanzas, that appear in the
autograph but not in the printed libretto (Apelle's aria in Act II,
Scene 7, first stanza; Campaspe's aria in Act II, Scene 9, second
stanza; Alessandro's aria in Act III, Scene 10, second stanza; and
Statira's aria in Act III, Scene 12, second stanza). Note that none
of these stanzas agrees with any of the stanzas in this category that
appear in the Cardiff and London scores, but not in the printed
libretto.

3) Aria texts from the autograph that appear in the printed libretto and the complete scores, but are set to different music in
INc (Alessandro's aria in Act II, Scene 7; Oronte's aria in Act III,
Scene 15). It will be recalled that, in the autograph, the original
text of Alessandro's aria had been crossed out and replaced by
another; yet it is the cancelled text that appears in the printed
libretto, in the scores, and in INc.

The existence of the aria collection at Naples raises questions
and invites speculation. As stated above, the Naples manuscript
contains settings of texts from complete scenes in the autograph
that were cut from the printed libretto, settings of stanzas that
appear only in the autograph, and, in two cases, different musical
settings of texts that appear both in the autograph and in the
printed libretto. Obviously, the composer of the music in INc
must have had access to the autograph. Because much of the music
in INc agrees with that preserved in the scores of the opera, one
can assume that Scarlatti was the composer of all the music found

there. Such a hypothesis is further supported by the fact that
there are no known performances of Scarlatti's *La Statira* after
those given in Rome in 1690; thus there seems little possibility
that other, later composers might have contributed to the work.
If one were to proceed on this assumption and consider the facts
we do know, one would arrive inevitably to the conclusion that
Scarlatti prepared a version of *La Statira* which was changed short-
ly before the first performance of the opera.

It was common practice to continue revising an opera from the
time of its conception until the final rehearsals. Indeed, alterations
continued to be made throughout the life of an opera on the stage.
The first performance of *La Statira* took place on the evening of
January 5, 1690, and the libretto bears the imprint 1690. The libretto was perhaps printed earlier—but not much earlier—during
the final weeks of 1689. In any case, the unnumbered pages of
textual material added at the end of the libretto clearly show that
changes were made after the body of the libretto had been printed.
Ottoboni finished the autograph libretto in March 1689. At that
time, Innocent XI was still alive, and none of the Ottoboni family
could have known of—or even guessed at—the dramatic events that
were to occur later in the year. Because of Innnocent's attitude
toward the theater, there was little hope in March of a public performance of Ottoboni's opera. It is possible that Ottoboni did not
consider a musical setting of his work until mid-October, when his
granduncle became Alexander VIII; this was less than three
months before the first performance of *La Statira*. On the other
hand, Scarlatti may have composed the opera earlier, in expecta-
tion of private performances; indeed, this is how the majority of
operatic productions were staged in seventeenth-century Rome.
Were this the case, it would help explain the existence of text and
music for Diana, which could have been added after it became
possible to perform the opera in a large public theater rather than
privately.

At present, it is impossible to determine the date when Ottoboni first approached Scarlatti to set his libretto, for no known
documents mention Ottoboni's negotiations with the composer.
Records do tell us, however, that Scarlatti was in Rome during
May, June, and part of July 1689. He had been hired as *maestro di*

cappella at the Neapolitan conservatory of Santa Maria di Loreto in February 1689 and asked his superiors for a month's leave of absence during May to go to Rome "for some business." By July 15, he still had not returned to Naples and he was summarily fired from his position.[11] By September, Scarlatti was back in Naples, and there is no record of his having returned to Rome before the end of the year. Whether or not the "business" that took him to Rome in late spring concerned *La Statira* is a matter of conjecture. In any case, the score must have been completed by late 1689.

It is probable that Scarlatti was not in Rome for the rehearsals of *La Statira* during the weeks immediately preceding its first performance and that, for whatever reasons, it was decided that last minute changes were necessary. Certain scenes, arias, and aria stanzas were apparently cut and others added. For example, the appearance of Diana in the final scene of the opera was added. According to the documents, it was originally planned to have Fame appear on a mechanical device singing the praises of the Ottoboni family, but Don Antonio, Cardinal Ottoboni's father, would not allow this. Such a scene does not appear in the autograph, which suggests that it, too, was a later thought. Another spectacular scene was then substituted, and this is the one we know from the added text in the printed libretto and from the scores. Because of the press of time, and because of Scarlatti's absence, it would have made sense to find a Roman composer, one known to Ottoboni, to write the new music required for this scene and for any other last-minute changes or additions.

Such a reconstruction of events becomes more than mere hypothesis thanks to the existence of two manuscript collections of arias, one in the Vatican Library (Chigi Q. IV. 37) and one in the Bibliothèque Nationale at Paris (Rés. Vmf. ms. 40).[12] The Chigi manuscript is a patched-together collection containing twelve arias, copied in the hands of at least two scribes. The first four are attributed to Francesco Gasparini; two of these, nos. 2 and 3, are from

---

[11] The document is quoted in Pagano and Bianchi, op. cit., p. 106.

[12] I should like to thank Professor Lowell Lindgren for drawing these manuscripts to my attention. He, Professor Margaret Murata, and Mlle. Catherine Massip of the Bibliothèque Nationale have supplied information about the arias in these collections.

Il Bellerofonte (Libretto by ? Conti, Rome, 1690). The eight remaining arias are all attributed to Flavio Carlo Lanciani. Nos. 5 and 12 are from *La forza del sangue* (libretto by Giovanni Andrea Lorenzani, Rome 1686). More importantly for our purposes, arias nos. 6 through 11, all copied in the same hand, are settings of texts from *La Statira*:

No. 6.	"Chi a volo troppo alto" (Alessandro, Act II, Scene 7), ff. 29-32v
No. 7.	"Dolce invidia" (Diana, Act III, Scene 16), ff. 33-35
No. 8.	"Tiranno, e che pretendi" (Alessandro, Act III, Scene 1), ff. 36-40v
No. 9.	"Crudo ciel, empio fato" (Oronte, Act I, Scene 3), ff. 41-46
No. 10.	"La clemenza nel cor" (Alessandro, Act I, Scene 11), ff. 47-53
No. 11.	"Viva pur l'arco e gli strali" (Diana, Act III, Scene 16), ff. 55-57v.

The manuscript in the Bibliothèque Nationale contains, among other pieces, six settings of texts from *La Statira*. The first five of these are attributed to Scarlatti, but the sixth carries the name of Lanciani:

"Mi consiglio col mio core" (Apelle, Act I, Scene 9), ff. 23-29

"Beltà che piace" (Campaspe, Act I, Scene 6), ff. 31-34v

"Ancor non so resolvermi" (Alessandro, Act I, Scene 12), ff. 35-42v

"Ho di selce la fortuna [= costanza] "(Oronte, Act I, Scene 1),

Act I, Scene 1), ff. 43-50v

"Son menzognieri instabili" (Campaspe, Act II, Scene 4), ff. 51-58v

"Esser potrai crudele (Apelle, Act II, Scene 2), ff. 120-127v

Flavio Carlo Lanciani (1661-1706), a composer and performer on the violone, violin, and keyboard, was a member of Cardinal Ottoboni's household from 1688 to 1699. Lanciani is known to have set a number of scared and secular librettos by Ottoboni, among them *L'amante del suo nemico* (Rome, 1688) and *Amore e graditudine* (Rome, 1690).[13] This latter opera, a pastorale, was performed a number of times in the fall of 1690, some six months after the final performances of *La Statira*. Given the close economic and artistic connections between Ottoboni and Lanciani, it is logical to suppose that it was Lanciani who was asked to compose additional music for the final version of *La Statira*. The texts, music, and attributions in the above-mentioned manuscript collections tend to support such a hypothesis.

Of the six arias attributed to Lanciani in Chigi Q. IV. 37, five are settings of texts not found in the autograph, although they appear in the printed libretto. No. 8 (one of Alessandro's two arias in Act III, Scene 1), no. 9 (Oronte's Act I, Scene 3 complete), and no. 10 (Alessandro's aria in Act I, Scene 11) are all printed in the body of the libretto. In each of these three instances, the added texts can be justified from a dramatic point of view: Act III, Scene 1 affords Alessandro yet another opportunity to display his confused emotions regarding the two women in his life; Act I, Scene 3, as pointed out earlier, both rounds out the dramatic situations that precede it and forms a connective link to the scene that follows; and, since Ottoboni decided to cut a pointless aria for Perinto in Act I, Scene 11, he took the opportunity to add another aria for Alessandro in that scene. This addition must have been decided upon at a very late date, for there is no indication of Ottoboni's intentions in the autograph as with another aria added to the libretto and the scores. Nos. 7 and 11 are the two arias for Diana in the closing scene of the opera, part of the text added at the end of the libretto.

---

[13] See note 3. For more information on Flavio Carlo Lanciani, see also Marx, op. cit., pp. 128 and 170; and G, Morelli, "Giovanni Andrea Lorenzani artista e letterato romano del seicento," *Studi secenteschi*, XIII (1972), pp. 198-201. Lanciani's dates here are taken from Morelli who supports them with documentary evidence. These differ from those given by H. J. Marx, "Lanciani, Flavio Carlo", in *The New Grove*, vol. 10, pp. 424-25.

The aria "Esser potrai crudele", attributed to Lanciani in the Paris manuscript, is a further indication of his important role in reworking the score of *La Statira*. As pointed out earlier, this is the sole instance in the opera where an autograph text is substituted by another in the printed libretto with no indication by Ottoboni in the autograph manuscript. The Paris version is unique in another way: unlike the garbled textual settings in all of the musical sources of the complete opera, it follows the printed text exactly.

One other text in Chigi Q. IV. 37 remains to be discussed: no. 6, "Chi a volo troppo alto." Here, as with all of the other arias in the Chigi manuscript, the music is the same as that in the complete scores of *La Statira*. As will be recalled, in the autograph this text was crossed out and replaced by another, yet it was the cancelled text which was set and printed in the final version of the libretto. The appearance of the aria in a different musical version in the Naples manuscript can be explained if one accepts the hypothesis that Scarlatti had prepared an earlier version of the opera. Stylistically, the setting in the Chigi manuscript (the one that has come down to us in the complete scores of the opera) is similar to the other arias attributed in the manuscript to Lanciani, especially the two simple continuo arias sung by Diana. These are quite different from the very elaborate setting of "Chi a volo troppo alto" in the Naples manuscript, which is filled with extended coloratura passages and accompanied by the full orchestra. Nevertheless, some questions remain that cannot be answered at this point. Why would Lanciani, working at a later time, not have set the substitute text in the autograph? Perhaps Ottoboni himself decided that the original, cancelled text was more appropriate. If so, why would Lanciani have composed music to a text that had already been set by Scarlatti? Bear in mind that all of the other texts in Chigi Q. IV. 37 are added texts—that is, texts that did not appear in the autograph. Furthermore, the Chigi setting of "Chi a volo troppo alto" is much simpler to perform than the setting in the Naples collection supposedly by Scarlatti. There was no apparent need to compose a less elaborate setting for Alessandro, since many of his other arias are quite ornate and difficult; Ottoboni's and Scarlatti's Alessandro did indeed have the vocal prowess needed for such pieces. Perhaps it was the singer himself who insisted on another setting of the text.

Not all of the texts added to the printed libretto are found in the Chigi manuscript. This is not surprising, for Chigi Q. IV. 37 is a patchwork collection of arias copied by different scribes. In all probability, portions of earlier manuscripts were lost before they were assembled and bound together in this collection. If this were the case, the six arias from *La Statira* attributed to Lanciani, all copied in the same hand, would represent only part of the music Lanciani composed for the opera. For example, the added text and music in Act III, Scene 5 (the love scene between Campaspe and Apelle) might well be by Lanciani.

Thus we conclude our investigation of the textual sources of *La Statira* and of the collaboration between librettist and composer. In the case of this collaboration—unlike those between Striggio and Monteverdi, Boito and Verdi, and Hofmannsthal and Strauss—there is no known correspondence between the two parties. It is therefore impossible to discuss their personal working relationship. [14] We do, however, have an autograph of the libretto, replete with additions, cancellations, and substitutions, as well as a single edition of a printed libretto. Purely musical considerations cannot be ignored, and the existence of music omitted in the complete scores as well as the attribution of some of the extant music to a composer other than Scarlatti complicates the picture, though not unduly. We have been concerned here primarily with the textual aspects of *La Statira*. A study of the text of the opera and of the many changes that were made in the work—from even before March 4, 1689, when Ottoboni finished at least one version of his autograph until January 5, 1690, when the opera was first performed—provides us with valuable insight into the actual creation and completion of a *dramma musicale* in late-seventeenth-century Rome. It also gives us a glimpse into the working habits of a poet/librettist who at the same time was a generous patron of the arts, a prince of the Church, and a practical man of the theater.

---

[14] For an enlightened look at a seventeenth-century collaboration of a different kind, between a composer and an impresario, see C. B. Schmidt, "An Episode in the History of Venetian Opera: The *Tito* Commission," *Journal of the American Musicological Society*, XXXI (Fall, 1978), pp. 442-66.

A Documentary Postscript

In 1690, the official carnival season ran from Friday, January 6, until Ash Wednesday, February 8. Easter fell on Sunday, March 26. Elaborate dramatic and musical entertainments had been planned by the various colleges as well as by many of the prominent nobility, among them G. B. Rospigliosi, Duke of Zagarolo; the Colonna and Altieri families; and the Spanish ambassador. Cardinal Ottoboni, because of his family connections with the new pope, had the privilege of opening the festivities with a sumptuous performance of *La Statira* at the Tordinona theater on Thursday, January 5, the eve of Epiphany. There are a number of extant sources documenting this and subsequent performances of *La Statira* during and after the carnival season. They are cited here not only as evidence, but also for the light they can throw on the workings of a society once again set free to follow its own devices after having been forced to curtail its activities for so many years under Innocent XI. The documents are:

Fas 3956	Florence, Archivio di Stato, Mediceo 3956. Roma e Stato della Chiesa. Lettere Abbate Mancini.
Fas 3408	Florence, Archivio di Stato, Mediceo 3408. Sig. Ab. Mancini, Lettere e Minuti.

MOas 67   Modena, Archivio di Stato, Busta 67[66]. Avvisi
[66]   di Roma.

MOas 259   Modena, Archivio di Stato, Cavalleria Ducale-Es-
           tero. Ambasciatori, Agenti e correspondenti Esten-
           si, Italia, Roma, Vol. 259. Carteggi dell'Abbate
           Panziroli.

Rvat   Biblioteca Apostolica Vaticana, Computisteria
           Ottoboni, Giustificazioni.
           Vol. 13 [1454]
           Vol. 14 [1451]
           Vol. 15 [1457]
           Vol. 18 [1458]
           Vol. 20 [1455]

After Christmas of 1689, theatrical performances could again be given, although carnival had not yet officially begun. Some of these performances are duly noted in reports from the Florentine agent, the Abbate Giovanni Battista Mancini:

Fas 3956 and 3408, letter of January 3, 1690

> Si continuano le commedie di Capranica, e
> presto si darà principio all'altre in
> musica e dell'istrione . . .
>
> *The performances at the Capranica theater are*
> *continuing, and soon others will begin, both*
> *sung and spoken . . .*

The very next reports from Rome speak of the first performances of *La Statira*; two were sent to Florence and two to Modena:

Fas 3956 and 3408, letter of January 7

> Giovedì sera si fece la commedia per la prima
> volta nel Teatro di Tor di Nona, opera del
> Sig. Cardinale Ottoboni che riuscì per scene,
> e abiti molto magnifica, ma parve malinconica
> assai, e vi fu un concorso grandissimo. . . .

*Thursday evening there was a première performance
at the Tordinona theater. [It was]
a work by Cardinal Ottoboni that achieved success
through its magnificent costumes and scenery,
but appeared very sad. There was a very large
attendance . . .*

MOas 67 [66], letter of January 7

Giovedî sera si fece per la prima volta la
Comedia di Tor di Nona e pare che generalmente
abbia applauso per la musica, per le scene e
per i musici, ma non gran cosa per le
parole. In fine della detta comedia do-
veva venire in una machina la Fama can-
tando lodi della Casa Ottoboni; ma don
Antonio si è opposto esortando a farli cantare
qualche altra cosa, et il figlio ha voluto
che non sia più la detta machina . . .

*Thursday evening there was a première perfomance
at the Tordinona theater, and it seems generally
that there was much applause for the music,
for the scenery, and for the singers, but not very
much for the text. At the end of the opera Fame
was to have appeared in a mechanical device
singing the praises of the Ottoboni family; but Don
Antonio opposed this, demanding that
something else be sung, and his son desired
that the machine no longer be used. . . .*

MOas 259, letter of January 11

. . . tra le altre opere che si sentono in
musica ha solo il grido quella del teatro
di Tordinona, nella quale recita il nostro Sig.
Borosini con applauso di essere il miglior
cantante di tutti, avendo anco la prima parte
che è l'*Oronte*; il drama glielo invio in

questo ordinario che si contenterà presentarlo
al Sig. Duca Serenissimo. . . .

*. . . among the other operas that are being
heard, only the one at the Tordinona
theater is being praised. In it is singing
our own Sig. Borosini, who is being lauded
as the best singer of all, and who has the
principal role of* Oronte. *I am sending the
drama to you with this mail so that you
will be pleased to present it to the Most
Serene Duke. . . .*

MOas 259, another letter of January 11

Riceverà l'A. [ltezza] V. [ostra] in questo
ord. [inario] il drama musicale nel quale
ha la prima parte il Borosini, che fa da
Oronte et è stimato tra tutti il miglior
cantante; l'opera ha grido e vien lodata
da tutti. . . .

*Your Highness will receive in this mail the
musical drama in which Borosini sings the
principal role; he sings* Oronte *and is
held to be the best among all of the
singers. The opera is successful and is
praised by everybody. . . .*

A number of interesting facts can be gleaned from these letters.
The Tordinona theater, long closed, was refurbished at great expense, and *La Statira* was mounted for its reopening. According to
the correspondents, the music, the singers, and the scenery were
greatly admired. One also learns, however, that the subject was
thought to be rather sad for the joyous carnival season, and that
the libretto was considered the weakest element of the work. A bit
of subtle politicking is apparent in the letters from the Modenese
correspondents. Both reports make it clear that the tenor Antonio

Borosini was the most praised of all the singers.[15] At that time Borosini had connections with the court of Modena, and such statements would, of course, flatter the duke. The part of Oronte, though an important one, is hardly the principal role in the opera. As regards the "drama" sent to the duke, the letters are not clear. Perhaps it was a copy of the libretto. If it were a copy of the score, however, this might explain why the title of *Oronte* appears on the spine of the Modenese copy of *La Statira*, as mentioned earlier.

The report of a mechanical device carrying Fame to sing the praises of the Ottoboni family is intriguing. Surely, Cardinal Ottoboni must have known of this—and perhaps even planned it himself. His father, Don Antonio, the nephew of Alexander VIII, was of another mind and opposed the introduction of such obvious obsequiousness. The fact that an Alexander—and a magnanimous Alexander at that—was one of the principal characters in the opera was flattery enough. The addition of music and text for Diana, attributed to Lanciani, was obviously the alternative solution.

A shadow was cast over carnival festivities, but it lasted only a few days:

Fas 3956 and 3408, letter of January 14

> Mercoledî sera proibirono tutte le commedie
> eccetto quella del Teatro Tor di Nona, ma
> giovedî sera poi le restituirono. . . .
>
> *Wednesday evening all performances were*
> *probhibited except for that at the*
> *Tordinona theater, but Thursday evening*
> *they were reinstated. . . .*

Naples had been in the throes of the plague, and the Roman authorities were afraid that it might spread. Hence they forbade public theatrical performances. As can be seen in these letters, however, the performance of the cardinal's opera was exempted

---

[15] The tenor Antonio Borosini (ca. 1660-?) spent time in the service of Francesco I at Modena, although he sang in many other places, principally at Hanover and Vienna. See the biographical entry by C. Casellato in *Dizionario biografico degli italiani*, vol. 12, pp. 806-807.

from the prohibition. It played as scheduled on Wednesday the eleventh.

The next performance of *La Statira* took place on Tuesday, January 24. The reports to the court at Modena give us further information about the singers.

MOas 259, letter of January 25

> Fui ieri sera alla commedia di Tordinona la quale merita di esser lodata quanto al teatro, scene, vestiti e accompagnamenti proprissimi; e li musici hanno pure qualche applauso come il contralto di V.[ostra] A.[ltezza] Pasqualino et anco Mont'Alcino. . . .

> *Yesterday evening I was at the performance at the Tordinona theater, one that deserves praise for the stage, scenery, costumes, and very appropriate properties. The singers also receive some applause, as for instance Your Highness's contralto Pasqualino and also Mont'Alcino. . . .*

MOas 259, another letter of January 25

> La commedia o sia opera in musica, composta nelle parole da card. Ottobono, è piacciuta molto: vi fui hieri sera e nelle scene, vestiti, accompagnamenti si può lodare infinitamente quanto si possa mai quelle di Venezia in questo genere. . . .

> *The play, or opera, composed to the words of Cardinal Ottoboni, has given great pleasure: I was there yesterday evening, and it can be infinitely praised for its scenery, costumes, and properties as much as anything of its kind in Venice. . . .*

Since Venice, with its many theaters, continued to enjoy pre-eminence in the production of operas, it was indeed a compliment to compare the production of *La Statira* with those in Venice.

The two singers mentioned were among the most famous of their day. Both Pasqualino Thiepoli da Udine and Bartolomeo Monaci da Mont'Alcino were members of Ottoboni's household and later became attached to the pontifical chapel.

Only a little information is known about the singers who took part in the performances of *La Statira* and the roles they sang. As mentioned earlier, Antonio Borosini, a tenor, sang Oronte. Thiepoli and Mont'Alcino cannot be so easily cast. Thiepoli is known to have sung exclusively as a soprano, while Mont'Alcino sang both soprano and alto parts. Yet the Modenese correspondent refers to Thiepoli as a "contralto." It is possible that the writer confused the singers in his letter, in which case it would have been Mont'Alcino who sang the role of Statira while Thiepoli sang one of the other principal soprano roles (Alessandro or Campaspe). If the Modenese correspondent was correct in his report, however, then Thiepoli sang Statira. One other singer can be assigned a role in the opera: the soprano Giuseppe Ceccarelli, also known as Peppino. He undoubtably sang the role of Perinto, for he is listed as having been costumed for that role in the bills for later performances of *La Statira* at the Cancelleria (see below).[16]

Aside from the threat of plague, there were other events in Rome itself that did not bode well for the various theatrical activities taking place during the carnival of 1690.

Fas 3956, letter of January 31

> Nostro Signore sta con ottima salute dando
> continue udienze e qua non si attende ad
> altro che a fare un bel carnovale con maschere
> e comedie, quella però fatta dal Sig. Amba-
> sciatore di Spagna ha portato, e porta l'applau-
> so universale sopra tutte le altre che sono
> in musica . . .

[16] For information on Ceccarelli (?-1733), Mont'Alcino (?-1737), and Thiepoli (ca. 1670-1742) see Marx, op. cit., pp. 165, 173, and 176, respectively.

Il tempo piovoso di ieri impedî gran parte
delle maschere, si corse però il palio . . .
Si sta con grandissima paura che non siano per
nascere delle inconvenienze e a quest'effetto
fanno diligenze grandissime et insolite e a
tutte le comedie che si fanno mettono soldate
alle porte e si vede evidentement che il
popolaccio non è sodisfatto di questo
governo . . .

The Holy Father is in the best of health,
giving continual audiences, and no one thinks
of anything else but having a fine carvnival
with masks and plays. But the one given by
the Spanish ambassadore has had, and
continues to have the greatest success,
more than all the rest that are set to
music. . . .
The rainy weather yesterday kept in many
of the maskers, but the palio was run any-
way. . . . There is a great fear that there will
be unrest, and for this reason they are
taking great and unusual precautions. At
all theatrical performances they are placing
soldiers at the doors, and one sees clearly
that the common people are not satisfied
with the government. . . .

Apparently there was thought to be danger of civil unrest, but the
fears must have been allayed, for nothing more is mentioned about
the matter during the remainder of the carnival season. The letter
also alludes to an opera given by the Spanish ambassador, the
Marquis Coccogliudo, at the Colonna palace. The *Avvisi* first mention the work in a dispatch written on January 17 (Fas 3956),
and the work continues to appear in the *Avvisi* throughout carnival season. The opera in question is *La Caduta del regno dell' Ama-
zoni* (libretto by Giovanni de Totis, music by Bernardo Pasquini).
There can be little doubt that this opera—and not *La Statira*—was
the most successful of the season.

The final performance of *La Statira* given during carnival proper took place on Monday, February 6, and was an occasion for other festivities as well.

MOas 67 [66], letter of February 4

> Si dice che il card. Ottoboni domani [*sic*]
> a sera finita la comedia nel teatro di
> Tordinona si farà un festino. Avendo monsù
> Arimbert rappresentato di rimetter molto
> nella comedia, ha ottenuto di far recitare
> una rappresentazione a quaresima, se sarà
> a ordine o pure a Pasqua per rinfrancarsi. . .

> *It is said that Cardinal Ottboni will hold*
> *a reception at the Tordinona theater to-*
> *morrow [sic] night after the performance*
> *is finished. Monsieur Alibert, having*
> *pointed out that he spent much on the*
> *opera, has obtained permission to give a*
> *performance during Lent, if that is in*
> *order, or at Easter, so that he might*
> *recoup his expenses. . . .*

This report is of great interest, for it contains the first public announcement of the lavish party with entertainment that was to be given at the theater by Prince Antonio Ottoboni, the cardinal's father, after the final performance of the opera during carnival. Furthermore, the letter hints at the financial problems that must have beset the production of *La Statira*. The Frenchman Jacques (Giacomo in Italian) d'Alibert was the man who had first opened the Tordinona theater in 1671.[17] At that time he had been in partnership with Queen Christina of Sweden, then resident in Rome. D'Alibert was also in charge of reopening the theater for the carnival season of 1690. This time, however, he operated in association with Ottoboni, for Christina had died in 1689. Unfortunately for d'Alibert, there were to be no further performances of

[17] For details of d'Alibert's life and career, see Cametti, op. cit., *passim*.

La Statira at the Tordinona theater. As we shall see, they took place elsewhere in the city.

The *festino* given on February 6 was an elaborate and very expensive effort, as the many surviving bills connected with it confirm.[18] The reports all take pains to mention the *festino*, some in more detail than others.

Fas 3956, letter of February 7

> Qua poi si è finito il Carnovale con numero infinito di maschere . . . e vi è stato gran numero de' festini nelli quali le dame si son pure sfogate, e un' sera doppo la comedia del Sig. Cardinale Ottobono nel Teatro di Tor di Nona fu fatto un bellissmo festino di dame con grandissimo concorso de' cardinali e vi fu anche de' molti francesi. . .

> *Here carnival has ended with an infinite number of masked balls . . . and there have been a great many parties which the ladies have enjoyed. And one evening after Cardinal Ottoboni's opera in the Tordinona theater a most beautiful reception was given for the ladies with many cardinals in attendance. There were also many Frenchmen. . . .*

Fas 3408, letter of February 7

> . . . e ieri sera doppo la comedia del Sig. Card. Ottobono nel Teatro di Trodinona fu fatto un bellissimo festino di Dame. . . .

> *. . . and yesterday evening after Cardinal Ottoboni's opera at the Tordinona theater a most beautiful* festino *was given, with the ladies present . . .*

---

[18] Rvat 13, Quinternetto 158 contains many bills pertaining to the preparations.

MOas 259, letter of February 8

> Lunedî sera dopo la recita dell'opera nel
> teatro di Tordinona il sig. D. Antonio diede
> un regalatissimo rinfresco che servî anco
> per una lautissima cena a tutte le dame e
> cavalieri chi vi volsero intervenire e dopo
> questa nello stesso teatro adobato quel
> piano ad arazzi si fece una bellissima festa,
> uscendo prima fuori del teatro una machina
> entro la quale apparvero tutti li sonatori
> di diversi instromenti che formarono
> l'orchestra. . . .

> *Monday evening after the performance of the*
> *opera at the Tordinona theater, Don Antonio*
> *gave a magnificent reception which also in-*
> *cluded a sumptuous supper for all the ladies*
> *and gentlemen who cared to attend. After*
> *this in the theater itself, which was decorated*
> *with tapestries, there was a gorgeous enter-*
> *tainment that began with the appearance from*
> *the stage of a mechanical device upon which were*
> *all the instrumentalists who made up the or-*
> *chestra. . . .*

This reception caused a sensation. It was arranged "in the Venetian manner," and apparently was the first of its kind to have taken
place in Rome. A French traveller who was present, the Marquis
de Coulanges, gives a detailed description in his memoires:[19]

> Le prince Antonio Ottoboni donna aussi aux
> dames romaines une fête à la mode de son pays,
> c'est-à-dire de Venise; elle fut pour Rome un
> spectacle nouveau et qui réussit très agréable-
> ment. Le dernier jour du carnaval qu'on

[19] *Mémoires de M. de Coulanges* (Paris, 1820). This passage is reprinted in
A. Ademollo, *I Teatri di Roma durante il secolo decimosettimo* (Rome,
1888), pp. 179-180.

représenta sur le théâtre public de
Tordinona le grand opéra, le parterre, fermé
au public, fut disposé en salle de bal.
Aussitôt, que l'opéra fut fini, toutes les
personnes considérables qui voulurent
danser descendirent des loges par un escalier
à deux rampes qui avoit été pratiqué exprès,
et qui ajoutoit encore à la beauté de la
décoration. Dans le même moment il descendit
insensiblement du plafond de la salle une
infinitê de bougies allumées dans chandeliers
de cristal, et l'on alluma encore des flambeaux
de poing de cire blanche qui étoient disposés
entre chaque loge depuis le haut jusqu'en bas.

La compagnie ne fut pas plutôt placée, que la
toile du théâtre se revela, et l'on découvrit au
fond une troupe de masques placée sur une
espèce d'amphithéâtre qui se détacha et vint
insensiblement jusqu'à bord du théâtre; il s'y
arrêta, et les premiers coups d'archet firent
reconnôitre la meilleure symphonie de Rome.
Alors le bal commença par une marche lente et
grave d'"hommes et de femmes, deux à deux, qui
dura assez long-temps, et qui avoit bien plus de
l'air d'une procession que d'un branle. Le prince
de Turenne étoit à la tête; il donnoit la main à
la princesse Ottoboni, femme de don Antonio.

Ils étoient suivis de tous les seigneurs et
dames, conformément au cérémonial romain.
Tous les cardinaux, prélats, ambassadeurs,
et ceux qui ne vouloient point danser, étoient
restés dans les loges, d'où l'on voyoit à
son aise cette belle assemblée. A cette
première marche si grave en succédèrent d'autres
un peu moins sérieuses, qui se terminèrent par
nos menuets français, qu'on dansa, tant bien
que mal, en faveur de la duchesse Lanti, du

prince de Turenne et des étrangers curieux de
nos manières et de nos modes. Pendant le
bal, on présenta grand nombre de corbeilles
remplies de fruits et de confitures, et toutes
sortes de rafraîchissements avec
profusion.

*Prince Antonio Ottoboni also offered to the
ladies of Rome a reception in the manner of
his native city, that is, Venice; it was
a new spectacle for Rome and was very successful. On the final day of carnival the*
parterre *of the public Tordinona theater where
they are performing the huge opera was closed
to the public and arranged as a ballroom.
After the performance was finished, any of the
great number of people who wished to dance
descended from their boxes on a double stair-
case, made especially for the occasion, and
which added still more to the beauty of the
scene. At this moment there quietly descended
from the ceiling of the theater a great number
of lighted candles in crystal chandeliers;
further illumination was provided by
large candles of white wax that were placed
between each box, from the topmost to the
lowest.*

*The people were hardly in their places when the
curtain of the stage rose, revealing at the
back a number of masked people on a type of
amphitheater which imperceptibly moved toward
the front of the stage. It stopped there,
and the first drawing of the bows of the
violins revealed the best orchestra in Rome.
Then the ball began with a slow and grave
march of ladies and gentlemen walking in twos,
which lasted a very long time and had more the
air of a procession than a* branle. *The Prince*

> *of Turenne was at its head, and he gave his*
> *hand to the Princess Ottoboni, wife of Don*
> *Antonio.*
>
> *They were followed by all the ladies and*
> *gentlemen, in accordance with Roman protocol.*
> *All of the cardinals, prelates, ambassadors,*
> *and those who did not want to dance remained*
> *in their boxes, from which they could watch*
> *the splendid company at their ease. After this*
> *opening piece, which was so grave, there*
> *followed others somewhat less serious. These*
> *finished with our French minuets, which were*
> *danced, for better or for worse, for the*
> *pleasure of the Duchess Lanti, the Prince of*
> *Turenne, and for foreigners who were curious*
> *about our customs and fashions. During the ball,*
> *we were offered baskets of fruits and sweets, and*
> *a profusion of refreshments.*

Then came Lent and, with it, the traditional cessation of all theatrical activity. It appears, however, that during the short pontificate of Alexander VIII Rome was hardly tradition-minded.

Fas 3956 and 3408, letter of February 28

> Il Sig. Card. Ottobono domenica doppo pranzo
> fece sotto titolo d'oratorio una rappresenta-
> zione intitolata Il Martirio di Sant'
> Eustachio con balletti e mutazioni de scene . . .

> *On Sunday after dinner Cardinal Ottoboni,*
> *calling it an oratorio, had a performance*
> *of* Il martirio di Sant'Eustachio, *complete*
> *with dancing and changes of scenery. . . .*

Fas 3956 and 3408, letter of March 7

> Si è fatta per tre sere in Cancelleria la
> rappresentazione di Sant'Eustachio, e
> questa sera si deve rifare la comedia del

Sig. Ambasciatore di Spagna. . . .

La comedia del Sig. Ambasciatore di Spagna
si è diferita a farsi a sabbato per esser
ammalato il musico che ha la parte principale. . . .

Sant'Eustachio *has been performed for*
three evenings at the Cancelleria, and
this evening the opera at the Spanish
ambassador's is to be done again. . . .

The opera at the Spanish ambassador's
has been postponed until Saturday because
the singer who has the principal role
is ill. . . .

Fas 3956, letter of March 14

Sabbato il Sig. Ambasciatore di Spagna volse
rifare la sua comedia ma nostro signore si
lasciò intendere che non era di sua
soddisfazione che si facesse in questo tempo,
e si è diferita per farla l'ottava di pasque. . . .

Saturday the Spanish ambassador wanted to
perform his opera again, but the Holy
Father let it be known that it did not
please him to have it presented at this
time, so it has been postponed until
the week after Easter. . . .

Not only did Cardinal Ottoboni present *Il Martirio di Sant'Eustachio*, a sacred oratorio, as a staged work, but the Spanish ambassador held further performances of *La caduta del regno dell'Amaz-
zoni*. If the former were not enough to provoke the pope to action, certainly the latter was, and performances of the opera were
suspended. No further performances of any kind are recorded for
the remainder of Lent.

Earlier, Ottoboni had planned to continue performances of *La
Statira* after Easter, but privately at the Cancelleria rather than at
the Tordinona theater. Thus preparations were made:

Rvat 13, fasc. 180, February 20

> Pagato quattro facchini che hanno portato
> le dui mute di scene dal Teatro di Tor di
> Nona alla Cancelleria . . .

> *Paid: four porters who carried the two*
> *changes of scenery from the Tordinona*
> *theater to the Cancelleria. . . .*

Rvat 15, fasc. 648, April 9

> A dì 9 Aprile 1690. All. Emm:^{o} e R:^{mo} Sig.^{re}
> Cardinal D. Pietro Ottoboni. Robbe date per
> servitio della Commedia di Statira in
> Cancelleria. . . .

> *The 9th day of April, 1690. To the Most*
> *Eminent and Reverend Cardinal Don Pietro*
> *Ottoboni. Materials given for use in the*
> *opera* Statira *at the Cancelleria. . . . [Then*
> *follow three pages listing costume materials*
> *for all of the characters in the opera. Some*
> *of these are entered by the character's name*
> *and some by the singer's name. The bill is*
> *countersigned by Ottoboni's maestro di casa,*
> *Arcangelo Spagna.]*

Thus, sets were transferred from the theater to the palace not long after the beginning of Lent, and apparently new costumes were ordered for the performances at the Cancelleria. Note that only two changes of scenery—many fewer than the opera originally called for—were transported to the small makeshift stage. Many of the sets and all of the costumes of the original production remained at the Tordinona theater, then, as d'Alibert's property. Perhaps this was done to aid his precarious financial position and to compensate him for the lack of further performances of the opera at his theater.

D'Alibert was not the only one who ran up exorbitant expenses during the carnival season and afterward.

Ad 9 Aprile 1690

All'Em[inentissi]mo e R[everendissi]mo Sig[nor] Cardinal D. Pietro Ottobon[i]

Robbe date a Servitio della Commedia di Statira in Cancelleria

Para V[n]a Calzette di Seta d'Inghilterra color di fiore...
...di Statira
Para V[n]a detto Simile d'Inghilterra d'Appelle...
Para V[n]a detta Simile Gialle...
Para V[n]a calzone di Seta di Parma Inca[rnato]...
V[n]a Para di Paggio che Cantà...
Para Calzette di Seta di Napoli per le Damigelle che
Rapresentano le persian[e] Para Dui
Para quattro Calzette di Seta di Parma...
Canne Sette ¾ saruscia di francia...
...blù di Genivero...
Canne...6 detta torchina e bianca per le maniche
d'Appelle...
Canne quattro ... saruscia torchina doppia...
...e spada d'Appelle...
Canne Nove ¾ Amarante Bianca...
Canne Sette e dui Bianca e color d'oro...
Canne V[n]a e ¾ detta simile Verde e bianca...
V[n]a Cinta...
Canne V[n]a e ¾ detta color di Rosa e bianca...
una Cinta di Statira...

CO = 20
D: ...½
L: ...½
L: 135
D: ...
D: ...½
— 50
— 50
L CO = 67

Ill. 5. List of costume materials, and their cost, for performances of *La Statira* given at the Cancelleria in April, 1690, 3 pages (Biblioteca Apostolica Vaticana, Ottob. Lat. 15, fasc. 648).

Canne quattordici ℔ 4 ferruccia da Cavaliere Inca.ta

Canne quattro e ℔ m 1½ detta bianca . . . .

Canne dodici negra da stringhe . . . .

Canne cinque torchina . . . .

Canne vinti cinque ferruccia da manto Inca.ta d.m

Canne quattro ferruccia forte Incarnata

Canne dodici e mezzo ferruccia rasata torchina

Canne dodici e mezzo detta Incarnata

Canne quindici detta d'argento ℔ . . . del moro

Canne quattro ferruccia d'argenticola nera

Canne sei e ℔ 5 merletto di filo bianco di fiandra
e cinque para di maniche di scavira appelle
Demetrio e Oronte aguili 16 Laca

Canne tre ℔ 4 ½ detto simile e le dui givelli del
Alito di scavira aguili 10 Laca

Canne tre ℔ 5½ detto piccolo e le spalle d'avanti

Canne dui ℔ m 1½ merletto di filo bianco ordinario
di milano a libra e detta e l'altro di Firenze

Canne una e ℔ m 1 merletto di vela concorsa fio a
℔ sola canna

Un collaro di merletto di Mezzo punto bianco
e scavira guarnito di ferruccia

Canne tre ℔ 6 velo bianco di Bologna

Canne dui e ℔ m 3½ Taffeta Incarnato e Limone
di Roma e tre para di Sottofabioli cioè uno
e Peppino e l'altro Demetrio e l'altro Oronte

Canne Una Barbantina e fodera — — — — — — — — — — 1:10

Palmi Dui e mezzo bombasina Gianchi e ore Crouate
è fattura e detti . . . . — — — — 60

Quattro dozinge di Seta Colorata e allaciare — — — — — 25

Dieci dette di fil[i] 4 e Struca letti — — — — — — 4 gn

e tre Cento Spillon - — — — — — — — — — — — — 06

Canne Sei fil[i] taffeta nero e Cinque Vestiti
e Ligeuri con il Portoghesino — — — — — — — 6:1/2

Canne Una Palmi ore Velo nero di bologna e dei
mori . . . . — — — — — — — — 55

Canne oro mi[o] e fornuia fotte n°5 e rimettere
al Abito d'Peppino — — — — — — — — — 12:4/2

Un Simiero con piume di piu colori — — — — —

Un Barrezone novo con piuma e Appelle } 13 —

e piu Canne quattro è mezzo fornuia di porzo
fino e la festa di scarira — — — — — 1: 030

iff[e] d'Fran d'Spagnia mio J. 10 par. 26:60
Sones fu fatt aro d'accordo e non estat
pagato, e quanos 101:63 a N.S. perche sonia
50:00 i mras sigare e la
26.60 piu J fin d'no Lonergo —
= 96:4 Fran Miuol —

Per fudi nominoncei va J. 40
importa il fino Conto dinoua sessei e
Arcangelo Gragna Tio d'Casa

MOas 67 [66], letter of March 22

> Il detto Cardinale Ottoboni ha già fatto
> un quantità di miglaia di scudi di debito
> spesi in mobili, in musici . . . oltre alla
> comedia nella quale ha pagate quattro parti
> principali, e nell'oratorio. . . .

> *The above-mentioned Cardinal Ottoboni has*
> *already incurred a debt of some thousands*
> *of scudi, spent on furnishings and on*
> *singers . . . in addition to the opera, for*
> *which he paid the singers of the four*
> *principal roles, as well as the oratorio. . . .*

In spite of these debts, plans for further performances of *La Statira* progressed.

There are records of three more performances of the opera after Easter: on April 9 (Fas 3956, letters of April 8 and April 11; Fas 3408, letter of April 11; MOas 259, letter of April 12), April 16 (Fas 3056 and 3408, letters of April 15, April 18, and April 22), and April 19 (MOas 67[66], letter of April 22). Although these reports mention the performances only in passing, two sections in them are of interest because of the unusual information they provide.

Fas 3956 and 3408, letter of April 11

> Domenica sera il Sig. Card. Ottoboni fece
> rappresentare nella Cancelleria sotto titolo
> d'oratorio la comedia della Statira. . . .

> *Sunday evening at the Cancelleria Cardinal*
> *Ottoboni had the opera* Statira *performed,*
> *calling it an oratorio [!]. . . .*

Fas 3956 and 3408, letter of April 15

> Doman sera il Sig. Card. Ottoboni fa recitare
> nuovamente in Cancelleria la sua opera della
> Statira a titolo di trattenimento. . . .

> *Tomorrow night Cardinal Ottoboni will again*
> *present his opera* Statira *at the Cancelleria,*
> *with the title of an entertainment. . . .*

Why Ottoboni felt compelled to disguise his opera by other designations is difficult to fathom. Easter had passed, and it was perfectly in order to hold theatrical performances. Again, there may be some connection between this subterfuge and Count d' Alibert. Be that as it may, Ottoboni and d'Alibert remained on good terms, for Ottoboni's next opera, *Il Colombo*, was produced at the Tordinona theater in December 1690 and January 1691.

As a conclusion to this Postscript, I should like to cite a few documents dealing with the performance conditions at the Cancelleria and Cardinal Ottoboni's plans to change them.

MOas 67[66], letter of February 22

> Si è poi fatta riflessione, che non
> sia conveniente di fare la scritta
> rappresentazione nel Teatro di Tordinona,
> onde in luogo di questa il Card. O., che
> vuole qualche ricreazione di musica
> prepara di far cantare un' oratorio con il
> palco e scene nel gran Salone della
> Cancelleria. . . .
>
> *It was then realized that it would not*
> *be convenient to give the planned*
> *performances at the Tordinona theater,*
> *wherefore in place of this Cardinal Ottoboni,*
> *who wants some musical recreation, is*
> *preparing to have an oratorio sung with*
> *a stage and scenery in the large reception*
> *room of the Cancelleria. . . .*

This report makes it clear that in the spring of 1690, to prepare for performances of the oratorio *Il martirio di Sant'Eustachio*, a stage was constructed in one of the large rooms in the palace.

Fas 3956 and 3408, letter of April 29

Il Sig. Card. Ottobono ha levate le stalle
del suo palazzo della Cancelleria e vi
fa un teatro da comedie molto superbo. . . .

Cardinal Ottoboni has torn down the
stables at the Cancelleria and is
building a superb theater there. . . .

MOas 67[66], letter of April 29

[Il Sig. Card. Ottoboni] . . . ha già fatto
dar principio alla fabrica d'un teatro
dentro il Palazzo della Cancelleria per
farvi recitare le comedie nel carnevale
furturo, et intende che questo succeda in luogo
di Tordinona, e che in quello recitino Istrioni
di prima riga. . . .

[Cardinal Ottoboni] . . . has already begun
construction of a theater behind the
palace of the Cancelleria in order to hold
performances there during the next carnival
season. And he wants this to be used instead
of the Tordinona, and to have performers of
the first rank there . . .

Although Ottoboni wanted the theater ready for the next season,
it was not to be. Before many years had passed, however, a per-
manent theater was in use at the palace. [20]

---

[20] The theater at the Cancelleria had a long and varied history and was rebuilt
many times. See A. Schiavo, *Il Palazzo della Cancelleria* (Rome, 1964),
pp. 183-192; and "Il teatro e altre opere del Cardinale Ottoboni," in *Strenna*
dei Romanisti (Rome, 1972), pp. 344-352. See also F. E. Warner, "The
Ottoboni Theater," *The Ohio State Theater Collection Bulletin*, XI (1964).

3B $\frac{a}{2}$